The Quest Series
Edited by G. R. S. Mead

RUYSBROECK

THE QUEST SERIES

Edited by G. R. S. MEAD,
EDITOR OF 'THE QUEST.'

Crown 8vo. 2s. 6d. net each.

FIRST LIST OF VOLUMES.

PSYCHICAL RESEARCH AND SURVIVAL. By JAMES H. HYSLOP, Ph.D., LL.D., Secretary of the Psychical Research Society of America.

THE QUEST OF THE HOLY GRAIL. By JESSIE L. WESTON, Author of 'The Legend of Sir Perceval.'

JEWISH MYSTICISM. By J. ABELSON, M.A., D.Lit., Principal of Aria College, Portsmouth.

THE MYSTICS OF ISLAM. By REYNOLD A. NICHOLSON, M.A., Litt.D., LL.D., Lecturer on Persian, Cambridge University.

BUDDHIST PSYCHOLOGY. By C. A. F. RHYS DAVIDS, M.A., Lecturer on Indian Philosophy, Manchester University.

RUYSBROECK. By EVELYN UNDERHILL, Author of 'Mysticism,' 'The Mystic Way,' etc.

THE SIDEREAL RELIGION OF THE ANCIENTS. By ROBERT EISLER, Ph.D., Author of 'Weltenmantel und Himmelszelt.' [*In the Press.*

LONDON: G. BELL AND SONS LTD.

RUYSBROECK

BY
EVELYN UNDERHILL
AUTHOR OF
'MYSTICISM,' 'THE MYSTIC WAY,' ETC., ETC.

LONDON
G. BELL AND SONS LTD.
1915

189.5
J33X
U55r

FOR

JESSIE

TO WHOM IT OWES SO MUCH

THIS LITTLE TRIBUTE TO A MUTUAL FRIEND

EDITOR'S NOTE

A GLANCE at the excellent Bibliographical Note at the end of the volume will reveal the surprising paucity of literature on Ruysbroeck in this country. A single version from the original of one short treatise, published in the present year, is all that we possess of direct translation; even in versions from translation there is only one treatise represented; add to this one or two selections of the same nature, and the full tale is told. We are equally poorly off for studies of the life and doctrine of the great Flemish contemplative of the fourteenth century. And yet Jan van Ruusbroec is thought, by no few competent judges, to be the greatest of all the mediæval Catholic mystics; and, indeed, it is difficult to point to his superior. Miss Evelyn Underhill is, therefore, doing lovers not only of Catholic mysticism, but also of mysticism in general, a very real service by her monograph, which deals more satisfactorily than any existing work in English with the life and teachings of one of the most spiritual minds in Christendom. Her book is not simply a painstaking summary of the more patent generalities of the subject, but rather a deeply sympathetic entering into the mind of Ruysbroeck, and that, too, with no common insight.

PREFATORY NOTE

I owe to the great kindness of my friend, Mrs. Theodore Beck, the translation of several passages from Ruysbroeck's *Sparkling Stone* given in the present work; and in quoting from *The Twelve Béguines* have often, though not always, availed myself of the recently published version by Mr. John Francis. For all other renderings I alone am responsible.

E. U.

CONTENTS

CHAP.		PAGE
I.	RUYSBROECK THE MAN	1
II.	HIS WORKS	36
III.	HIS DOCTRINE OF GOD	52
IV.	HIS DOCTRINE OF MAN	66
V.	THE ACTIVE LIFE	94
VI.	THE INTERIOR LIFE: ILLUMINATION AND DESTITUTION	115
VII.	THE INTERIOR LIFE: UNION AND CONTEMPLATION	136
VIII.	THE SUPERESSENTIAL LIFE	164
	BIBLIOGRAPHICAL NOTE	187

Luce divina sopra me s' appunta,
penetrando per questa ond' io m' inventro ;
La cui virtù, col mio veder conguinta,
mi leva sopra me tanto, ch' io veggio
la somma essenza della quale è munta.
Quinci vien l' allegrezza, ond' io fiammeggio ;
perchè alla vista mia, quant' ella è chiara,
la chiarità della fiamma pareggio.

Par. xxi. 83.

[Divine Light doth focus itself upon me, piercing through that wherein I am enclosed; the power of which, united with my sight, so greatly lifts me up above myself that I see the Supreme Essence where from it is drawn. Thence comes the joy wherewith I flame; for to my vision, even as it is clear, I make the clearness of the flame respond.]

RUYSBROECK

CHAPTER I

RUYSBROECK THE MAN

The tree Igdrasil, which has its head in heaven and its roots in hell (the lower parts of the earth), is the image of the true man. . . . In proportion to the divine heights to which it ascends must be the obscure depths in which the tree is rooted, and from which it draws the mystic sap of its spiritual life.

COVENTRY PATMORE.

IN the history of the spiritual adventures of man, we find at intervals certain great mystics, who appear to gather up and fuse together in the crucible of the heart the diverse tendencies of those who have preceded them, and, adding to these elements the tincture of their own rich experience, give to us an intensely personal, yet universal, vision of God and man. These are constructive spirits, whose creations in the spiritual sphere sum up and represent the best achievement of a whole epoch; as in other spheres the great artist, musician, or poet—always the child of tradition as well as of inspiration—may do.

John Ruysbroeck is such a mystic as this. His career, which covers the greater part of the fourteenth century—that golden age of Christian mysticism—seems to exhibit within the circle of a single personality, and carry up to a higher term than ever before, all the best attainments of the Middle Ages in the realm of Eternal Life. Rooted firmly in history, faithful to the teachings of the great Catholic mystics of the primitive and mediæval times, Ruysbroeck does not merely transmit, but transfigures, their principles : making from the salt, sulphur, and mercury of their vision, reason, and love, a new and living jewel—or, in his own words, a ' sparkling stone '—which reflects the actual radiance of the Uncreated Light. Absorbing from the rich soil of the Middle Ages all the intellectual nourishment which he needs, dependent too, as all real greatness is, on the human environment in which he grows— that mysterious interaction and inter-penetration of personalities without which human consciousness can never develop its full powers—he towers up from the social and intellectual circumstances that conditioned him : a living, growing, unique and creative individual, yet truly a part of the earth from which he springs.

To speak of Ruysbroeck, as some enthusiastic biographers have done, as an isolated spiritual phenomenon totally unrelated to the life of his time, an 'ignorant monk' whose profound knowledge of reality is entirely the result of personal inspiration and independent of human history, is to misunderstand his greatness. The 'ignorant monk' was bound by close links to the religious life of his day. He was no spiritual individualist; but the humble, obedient child of an institution, the loyal member of a Society. He tells us again and again that his spiritual powers were nourished by the sacramental life of the Catholic Church. From the theologians of that Church came the intellectual framework in which his sublime intuitions were expressed. All that he does—though he does this to a degree perhaps unique in Christian history—is to carry out into action, completely actualise in his own experience, the high vision of the soul's relation to Divine Reality by which that Church is possessed. The central Christian doctrine of Divine Fatherhood, and of the soul's 'power to become the son of God': it is this, raised to the nth degree of intensity, experienced in all its depth and fullness, and demonstrated with the exactitude of a mathematician and the passion of a poet, which Ruysbroeck gives us. Thus tradition and authority, no less than the abundant inspiration, the direct ecstatic knowledge of God to which his writings bear witness, have their part in his achievement. His theological culture was wide and deep. Not only the Scriptures and the Liturgy, but St. Augustine, Dionysius the Areopagite, Richard of St. Victor, St. Bernard, St. Bonaventura, St. Thomas Aquinas, and many others have stimulated and controlled his thought; interpreting to him his ineffable adventures, and providing him with vessels in which the fruit of those adventures could be communicated to other men.

Nor is Catholic tradition the only medium through which human life has exercised a formative influence upon Ruysbroeck's genius. His worldly circumstances, his place within and reaction to the temporal order, the temper of those souls amongst which he grew—these too are of vital importance in relation to his mystical achievements. To study the interior adventures and formal teachings of a mystic without reference to the general trend and special accidents of his outer life, is to neglect our best chance of understanding the nature and sources of his vision of truth. The angle from which that vision is perceived, the content of the mind which comes to it, above all the concrete activities which it induces in the growing, moving, supple self: these are primary *data* which we should never ignore. Action is of the very essence

THE MAN

of human reality. Where the inner life is genuine and strong the outer life will reflect, however faintly, the curve on which it moves; for human consciousness is a unit, capable of reacting to and synthesising two orders, not an unresolved dualism—as it were, an angel and an animal—condemned to lifelong battle within a narrow cage.

Therefore we begin our study of Ruysbroeck the mystic by the study of Ruysbroeck the man : the circumstances of his life and environment, so far as we can find them out. For the facts of this life our chief authority will be the Augustinian Canon Pomerius, who was Prior and chronicler of Ruysbroeck's own community of Groenendael. Born in 1382, a year after Ruysbroeck's death, and entering Groenendael early in the fifteenth century, he knew and talked with at least two of the great mystic's disciples, John of Hoelaere and John of Scoonhoven. His life of Ruysbroeck and history of the foundation of the monastery was finished before 1420; that is to say, within the lifetime of the generation which succeeded the first founders of the house.[1] It represents the careful gathering up, sifting, and arranging of all that was remembered and believed by the community

[1] The *Vita* of Pomerius is printed in the *Analecta Bollandiana*, vol. iv. pp. 257 ff.

—still retaining several members who had known him in the flesh—of the facts of Ruysbroeck's character and career.

Pomerius was no wild romancer, but a reasonably careful as well as a genuinely enthusiastic monastic chronicler. Moderation is hardly the outstanding virtue of such home-made lives of monastic founders. They are inevitably composed in surroundings where any criticism of their subject or scepticism as to his supernatural peculiarities is looked upon as a crime ; where every incident has been fitted with a halo, and the unexplained is indistinguishable from the miraculous. Nevertheless the picture drawn by Pomerius—exaggerated though it be in certain respects—is a human picture ; possessed of distinct characteristics, some natural and charming, some deeply impressive. It is completed by a second documentary source : the little sketch by Ruysbroeck's intimate friend, Gerard Naghel, Prior of the Carthusian monastery of Hérines near Groenendael, which forms the prologue to our most complete MS. collection of his writings.

Ruysbroeck's life, as it is shown to us by Pomerius and Gerard, falls into three main divisions, three stages of ascent : the natural active life of boyhood ; the contemplative, disciplined career of his middle period ; the superessential life of supreme union which governed his existence at Groenendael. This course, which he trod in the temporal order, seems like the rough sketch of that other course trodden by the advancing soul within the eternal order—the Threefold Life of man which he describes to us in *The Adornment of the Spiritual Marriage* and other of his works.

Now the details of that career are these: John Ruysbroeck was born in 1293 at the little village of Ruysbroeck or Ruusbroec, between Brussels and Hal, from which he takes his name. We know nothing of his father; but his mother is described as a good and pious woman, devoted to the upbringing of her son—a hard task, and one that was soon proved to be beyond her. The child Ruysbroeck was strong-willed, adventurous, insubordinate; already showing signs of that abounding vitality, that strange restlessness and need of expansion which children of genius so often exhibit. At eleven years of age he ran away from home, and found his way to Brussels; where his uncle, John Hinckaert, was a Canon of the Cathedral of St. Gudule. Pomerius assures us that this escapade, which would have seemed a mere naughtiness in normal little boys, was in fact a proof of coming sanctity; that it was not the attraction of the city but a precocious instinct for the religious life— the first crude stirrings of the love of God—

which set this child upon the road. Such a claim is natural to the hagiographer; yet there lies behind it a certain truth. The little John may or may not have dreamed of being a priest; he did already dream of a greater, more enticing life beyond the barriers of use and wont. Though he knew it not, the vision of a spiritual city called him. Already the primal need of his nature was asserting itself—the demand, felt long before it was understood, for something beyond the comfortable world of appearance—and this demand crystallised into a concrete act. In the sturdy courage which faced the unknown, the practical temper which translated dream into action, we see already the germ of those qualities which afterwards gave to the great contemplative power to climb up to the ' supreme summits of the inner life ' and face the awful realities of God.

Such adventures are not rare in the childhood of the mystics. Always of a romantic temperament, endowed too with an abounding vitality, the craving for some dimly-guessed and wonderful experience often shows itself early in them; as the passion for music, colour or poetry is sometimes seen in embryo in artists of another type. The impact of Reality seems to be felt by such spirits in earliest childhood. Born susceptible in a special degree to the messages which pour in on man from the Transcendent, they move from the first in a different universe from that of other boys and girls; subject to experiences which they do not understand, full of dreams which they are unable to explain, and often impelled to strange actions, extremely disconcerting to the ordinary guardians of youth. Thus the little Catherine of Siena, six years old, already lived in a world which was peopled with saints and angels; and ruled her small life by the visions which she had seen. Thus the baby Teresa, mysteriously attracted by sacrifice, as other children are attracted by games and toys, set out to look for 'the Moors and martyrdom.' So too the instinct for travel, for the remote and unknown, often shows itself early in these wayfarers of the spirit; whose destiny it is to achieve a more extended life in the interests of the race, to find and feel that Infinite Reality which alone can satisfy the heart of man. Thus in their early years Francis, Ignatius and many others were restless, turbulent, eager for adventure and change.

This first adventure brought the boy Ruysbroeck to a home so perfectly fitted to his needs, that it might seem as though some secret instinct, some overshadowing love, had indeed guided his steps. His uncle, John Hinckaert, at this time about forty years of age, had lately been converted—it is said by a powerful sermon—from the comfortable and easy-going life of a prosperous ecclesiastic to the austere quest of spiritual perfection. He had distributed his wealth, given up all self-indulgence, and now, with another and younger Canon of the Cathedral named Francis van Coudenberg, lived in simplest, poorest style a dedicated life of self-denial, charity and prayer. He received his runaway nephew willingly. Perhaps he saw in this strange and eager child, suddenly flung upon his charity, an opportunity for repairing some at least amongst the omissions of his past—that terrible wreck of wasted years which torments the memory of those who are converted in middle life. His love and remorse might spend themselves on this boy. He might make of him perhaps all that he now longed to be, but could never wholly achieve: a perfect servant of the Eternal Goodness, young, vigorous, ardent, completely responsive to the touch of God.

Ruysbroeck, then, found a home soaked in love, governed by faith, renunciation, humility; a forcing-house of the spiritual life. In the persons of these two grown men, who had given up all outward things for the sake of spiritual realities, he was brought face to face—and this in his most impressionable years—with the hard facts, the concrete sacrifices, the heroic life of deliberate mortification, which underlay the lovely haunting vision, the revelation of the Divine beauty and love that had possessed him. No lesson is of higher value to the natural mystic than this. The lovers of Ruysbroeck should not forget how much they owe to the men who received, loved, influenced, educated the brilliant wayward and impressionable child. His attainment is theirs. His mysticism is rooted in their asceticism; a flower directly dependent for its perfection on that favouring soil. Though his achievement, like that of all men of genius, is individual, and transcends the circumstances and personalities which surround it; still, from those circumstances and personalities it takes its colour. It represents far more than a personal and solitary experience. Behind it lies the little house in Brussels, the supernatural atmosphere which filled it, and the fostering care of the two men whose life of external and deliberate poverty only made more plain the richness of the spirits who could choose, and remain constant to, this career of detachment and love.

The personal influence of Hinckaert and Coudenberg, the moral disciplines and perpetual self-denials of the life which he shared with them, formed the heart of Ruysbroeck's education; helping to build up that manly and sturdy character which gave its special temper to his mystical outlook. Like so many children destined to greatness, he was hard to educate in the ordinary sense ; uninterested in general knowledge, impatient of scholastic drudgery. Nothing which did not minister to his innate passion for ultimates had any attraction for him. He was taught grammar with difficulty ; but on the other hand his astonishing aptitude for religious ideas, even of the most subtle kind, his passionate clear vision of spiritual things, was already so highly developed as to attract general attention ; and his writings are sufficient witness to the width and depth of his theological reading. With such tastes and powers as these, and brought up in such a household, governed by religious enthusiasms and under the very shadow of the Cathedral walls, it was natural that he should wish to become a priest ; and in 1317 he was ordained and given, through the influence of his uncle, a prebend in St. Gudule.

Now a great mystic is the product not merely of an untamed genius for the Transcendent, but of a moral discipline, an interior education, of the most strenuous kind. All the varied powers and tendencies of a nature which is necessarily strong and passionate, must be harnessed, made subservient to this one central interest. The

instinctive egotism of the natural man—
never more insidious than when set upon
spiritual things—must be eradicated. So,
behind these few outward events of Ruysbroeck's adolescence, we must discern another growth; a perpetual interior travail,
a perpetual slow character-building always
going forward in him, as his whole personality
is moulded into that conformity to the vision
seen which prepares the way of union, and
marks off the mystical saint from the mere
adept of transcendental things. We know
from his writings how large a part such
moral purifications, such interior adjustments,
played in his concept of the spiritual life;
and the intimacy with which he describes
each phase in the battle of love, each step
of the spiritual ladder, the long process of
preparation in which the soul adorns herself
for the 'spiritual marriage,' guarantees to
us that he has himself trodden the path which
he maps out. That path goes the whole
way from the first impulse of 'goodwill,'
of glad acquiescence in the universal purpose, through the taming of the proud will
to humility and suppleness, and of the in-
surgent heart to gentleness, kindness, and
peace, to that last state of perfect charity
in which the whole spirit of man is one will
and one love with God.

Though his biographers have left us little
material for a reconstruction of his inner

development, we may surely infer something of the course which it followed from the vividly realistic descriptions in *The Kingdom of Lovers* and *The Spiritual Marriage*. Personal experience underlies the wonderful account of the ascent of the Spiritual Sun in the heavens of consciousness; the rapture, wildness and joy, the 'fever of love' which fulfils the man who feels its light and heat. Experience, too, dictates these profound passages which deal with the terrible spiritual reaction when the Sun declines in the heavens, and man feels cold, dead, and abandoned of God. Through these phases, at least, Ruysbroeck had surely passed before his great books came to be written.

One or two small indications there are which show us his progress on the mystic way, the development in him of those secondary psychic characters peculiar to the mystical type. It seems that by the time of his ordination that tendency to vision which often appears in the earliest youth of natural mystics, was already established in him. Deeply impressed by the sacramental side of Catholicism, and finding in it throughout his life a true means of contact with the Unseen, the priesthood was conceived by him as bringing with it a veritable access of grace; fresh power poured in on him from the Transcendent, an increase of strength wherewith to help the souls of other men. This belief took, in his meditations, a concrete and positive form. Again and again he saw in dramatic vision the soul specially dear to him, specially dependent on him—that of his mother, who had lately died in the Brussels Béguinage— demanding how long she must wait till her son's ordination made his prayers effectual for her release from Purgatory. At the moment in which he finished saying his first Mass, this vision returned to him; and he saw his mother's spirit, delivered from Purgatory by the power of the sacrifice which he had offered, entering into Heaven—an experience originating in, and giving sharp dramatic expression to, that sense of new and sacred powers now conferred on him, which may well at such a moment have flooded the consciousness of the young priest. This story was repeated to Pomerius by those who had heard it from Ruysbroeck himself; for " he often told it to the brothers."

For twenty-six years—that is to say, until he was fifty years of age—Ruysbroeck lived in Brussels the industrious and inconspicuous life of a secular priest. It was not the solitude of the forest, but the normal, active existence of a cathedral chaplain in a busy capital city which controlled his development during that long period, stretching from the very beginnings of manhood to the end of middle age; and it was in fact during these years, and in the midst of incessant distractions, that he passed through the great oscillations of consciousness which mark the mystic way. It is probable that when at last he left Brussels for the forest, these oscillations were over, equilibrium was achieved; he had climbed ' to the summits of the mount of contemplation.' It was on those summits that he loved to dwell, absorbed in loving communion with Divine Reality; but his career fulfilled that ideal of a synthesis of work and contemplation, an acceptance and remaking of the whole of life, which he perpetually puts before us as the essential characteristic of a true spirituality. No mystic has ever been more free from the vice of other-worldliness, or has practised more thoroughly and more unselfishly the primary duty of active charity towards men which is laid upon the God-possessed.

The simple and devoted life of the little family of three went on year by year undisturbed; though one at least was passing through those profound interior changes and adventures which he has described to us as governing the evolution of the soul, from the state of the ' faithful servant ' to the transfigured existence of the ' God-seeing man.' Ruysbroeck grew up to be a simple, dreamy, very silent and totally unimpressive person, who, 'going about the streets of Brussels with his mind lifted up into God,' seemed a nobody to those who did not know him. Yet not only a spiritual life of unequalled richness, intimacy and splendour, but a penetrating intellect, a fearless heart, deep knowledge of human nature, remarkable powers of expression, lay behind that meek and unattractive exterior. As Paul's twelve years of quiet and subordinate work in Antioch prepared the way of his missionary career; so during this long period of service, the silent growth of character, the steady development of his mystical powers, had gone forward in Ruysbroeck. When circumstances called them into play he was found to be possessed of an unsuspected passion, strength and courage, a power of dealing with outward circumstances, which was directly dependent on his inner life of contemplation and prayer.

The event into which the tendencies of this stage of his development crystallised, is one which seems perhaps inconsistent with the common idea of the mystical temperament, with its supposed concentration on the Eternal, its indifference to temporal affairs. As his childhood was marked by an exhibition of adventurous love, so his manhood was marked by an exhibition of militant love; of that strength and sternness, that passion for the true, which—no less than humility, gentleness, peace—is an integral part of that paradoxical thing, the Christian character.

The fourteenth century, like all great spiritual periods, was a century fruitful in mystical heresies as well as in mystical saints. In particular, the extravagant pantheism preached by the Brethren of the Free Spirit had become widely diffused in Flanders, and was responsible for much bad morality as well as bad theology; those on whom the 'Spirit' had descended believing themselves to be already divine, and emancipated from obedience to all human codes of conduct. Soon after Ruysbroeck came as a boy to Brussels, a woman named Bloemardinne placed herself at the head of this sect, and gradually gained extraordinary influence. She claimed supernatural and prophetic powers, was said to be accompanied by two Seraphim whenever she went to the altar to receive Holy Communion, and preached a degraded eroticism under the title of 'Seraphic love,' together with a quietism of the most exaggerated and soul-destroying type. All the dangers and follies of a false mysticism, dissociated from the controlling influence of tradition and the essential virtue of humility, were exhibited in her. Against this powerful woman, then at the height of her fame, Ruysbroeck declared war; and prosecuted his campaign with a violence and courage which must have been startling to those who had regarded him only as a shy, pious, rather negligible young man. The pamphlets which he wrote against her are lost; but the passionate denunciations of pantheism and quietism scattered through his later works no doubt have their origin in this controversy, and represent the angle from which his attacks were made.

Pantheists, he says in *The Book of Truth*, are "a fruit of hell, the more dangerous because they counterfeit the true fruit of the Spirit of God." Far from possessing that deep humility which is the soul's inevitable reaction to the revelation of the Infinite, they are full of pride and self-satisfaction. They claim that their imaginary identity with the Essence of God emancipates them from all need of effort, all practice of virtue, and leaves them free to indulge those inclinations of the flesh which the 'Spirit' suggests. They "believe themselves sunk in inward peace; but as a matter of fact they are deep-drowned in error."[1]

Against all this the stern, virile, ardent spirituality of Ruysbroeck opposed itself with its whole power. Especially did he hate and condemn the laziness and egotism of the quietistic doctrine of contemplation: the ideal of spiritual immobility which it

[1] *The Book of Supreme Truth*, cap. iv.

set up. That 'love cannot be lazy' is a cardinal truth for all real mystics. Again and again it appears in their works. Even that profound repose in which they have fruition of God, is but the accompaniment or preliminary of work of the most strenuous kind, and keeps at full stretch the soul which truly tastes it; and this supernatural state is as far above that self-induced quietude of 'natural repose'—"consisting in nothing but an idleness and interior vacancy, to which they are inclined by nature and habit"—in which the quietists love to immerse themselves, as God is above His creatures.

Here is the distinction, always needed and constantly ignored, between that veritable fruition of Eternal Life which results from the interaction of will and grace, and demands of the soul the highest intensity and most active love, and that colourable imitation of it which is produced by a psychic trick, and is independent alike of the human effort and the divine gift. Ruysbroeck in fighting the 'Free Spirit' was fighting the battle of true mysticism against its most dangerous and persistent enemy, — mysticality.

His attack upon Bloemardinne is the one outstanding incident in the long Brussels period which has been preserved to us. The next great outward movement in his steadily evolving life did not happen until the year 1343, when he was fifty years of age. It was then that the three companions decided to leave Brussels, and live together in some remote country place. They had long felt a growing distaste for the noisy and distracting life of the city; a growing dissatisfaction with the spiritual apathy and low level of religious observance at the Cathedral of St. Gudule; the need of surroundings in which they might devote themselves with total concentration to the contemplative life. Hinckaert and Coudenberg were now old men; Ruysbroeck was advanced in middle age. The rhythm of existence, which had driven him as a child from country to town, and harnessed him during long years to the service of his fellow-men, now drew him back again to the quiet spaces where he might be alone with God. He was approaching those heights of experience from which his greatest mystical works proceed; and it was in obedience to a true instinct that he went away to the silent places of the forest—as Anthony to the solitude of the desert, Francis to the 'holy mountain' of La Verna—that, undistracted by the many whom he had served so faithfully, he might open his whole consciousness to the inflow of the One, and receive in its perfection the message which it was his duty to transmit to the world. He went, says

Pomerius, "not that he might hide his light; but that he might tend it better and make it shine more brightly."

By the influence of Coudenberg, John III., Duke of Brabant, gave to the three friends the old hermitage of Groenendael, or the Green Valley, in the forest of Soignes, near Brussels. They entered into possession on the Wednesday of Easter week, 1343; and for five years lived there, as they had lived in the little house in Brussels, with no other rule save their own passion for perfection. But perpetual invasions from the outer world, not only of penitents and would-be disciples—for their reputation for sanctity grew quickly—but of huntsmen in the forest and pleasure parties from the town, who demanded and expected hospitality, soon forced them to adopt some definite attitude towards the question of enclosure. It is said that Ruysbroeck begged for an entire seclusion; but Coudenberg insisted that this was contrary to the law of charity, and that some at least of those who sought them must be received. In addition to these practical difficulties, the Prior of the Abbey of St. Victor at Paris had addressed to them strong remonstrances, on account of the absence of rule in their life and the fact that they had not even adopted a religious habit; a proceeding which in his opinion savoured rather of the ill-regulated doings of the heretical sects, than of the decorum proper to good Catholics. As a result of these various considerations, the simple and informal existence of the little family was re-modelled in conformity with the rule of the Augustinian Canons, and the Priory of Groenendael was formally created. Coudenberg became its provost, and Ruysbroeck, who had refused the higher office, was made prior; but Hinckaert, now a very old man in feeble health, refused to burden the young community with a member who might be a drag upon it and could not keep the full rigour of the rule. In a spirit of renunciation which surely touches the heroic, he severed himself from his lifelong friend and his adopted son, and went away to a little cell in the forest, where he lived alone until his death.

The story of the foundation and growth of the Priory of Groenendael, the saintly personalities which it nourished, is not for this place; except in so far as it affects our main interest, the story of Ruysbroeck's soul. Under the influences of the forest, of the silent and regular life, those supreme contemplative powers which belong to the 'Superessential Life' of Unity now developed in him with great rapidity. It is possible, as we shall see, that some at least of his mystical writings may date from his Brussels period; and we know that at the close of this period his reputation as an 'illuminated man' was already made. Nevertheless it seems safe to say that the bulk of his works, as we now possess them, represent him as he was during the last thirty years of his life, rather than during his earlier and more active career ; and that the intense certitude, the wide deep vision of the Infinite which distinguishes them, are the fruits of those long hours of profound absorption in God for which his new life found place. In the silence of the woods he was able to discern each subtle accent of that Voice which " is heard without utterance, and without the sound of words speaks all truth."

Like so many of the greatest mystics, Ruysbroeck, drawing nearer to Divine Reality, drew nearer to nature too ; conforming to his own ideal of the contemplative, who, having been raised to the simple vision of God Transcendent, returns to find His image reflected by all life. Many passages in his writings show the closeness and sympathy of his observation of natural things : the vivid description in *The Spiritual Marriage* of the spring, summer and autumn of the fruitful soul, the constant insistence on the phenomena of growth, the lessons drawn from the habits of ants and bees, the comparison of the surrendered soul to the sunflower, 'one of nature's most wonderful works'; the three types of Christians, compared with birds who can fly but prefer hopping about the earth, birds who swim far on the waters of grace, and birds who love only to soar high in the heavens. For the free, exultant life of birds he felt indeed a special sympathy and love; and 'many-feathered' is the best name that he can find for the soul of the contemplative ascending to the glad vision of God.

It is probably a true tradition which represents him as having written his greatest and most inspired pages sitting under a favourite tree in the depths of the woods. When the 'Spirit' came on him, as it often did with a startling suddenness, he would go away into the forest carrying his tablet and stylus. There, given over to an ecstasy of composition—which seems often to have approached the limits of automatic writing, as in St. Teresa, Boehme, Blake and other mystics—he would write that which was given to him, without addition or omission; breaking off even in the middle of a sentence when the 'Spirit' abruptly departed, and resuming at the same point, though sometimes after an interval which lasted several weeks, when it returned. In his last years, when eyesight failed him, he would allow a younger brother to go with him into the woods, and there to take down from dictation the fruits of those meditations in which he 'saw without sight'; as the illiterate Catherine of Siena dictated in ecstasy the text of her Divine Dialogue.

Two witnesses have preserved Ruysbroeck's solemn affirmation, given first to his disciple Gerard Groot 'in great gentleness and humility,' and repeated again upon his death-bed in the presence of the whole community, that every word of his writings was thus composed under the immediate domination of an inspiring power; that 'secondary personality of a superior type,' in touch with levels of reality beyond the span of the surface consciousness, which governs the activities of the great mystics in their last phases of development. These books are not the fruit of conscious thought, but 'God-sent truths,' poured out from a heart immersed in that Divine Abyss of which he tries to tell.

That a saint must needs be a visionary, is a conviction deeply implanted in the mind of the mediæval hagiographer; who always ascribes to these incidents an importance which the saints themselves are the first to deny. Pomerius thus attributes to Ruysbroeck not only those profound and direct experiences of Divine Reality to which his works bear witness; but also numerous visions of a conventional and anthropomorphic type, in which he spoke with Christ, the Blessed Virgin and the Saints, ecstasies

which fell upon him when saying Mass—
and the passionate devotion to the Eucharist
which his writings express makes these at
least probable—a certain faculty of clair-
voyance, and a prophetic knowledge of his
own death. Further, it is said that once,
being missed from the priory, he was found
after long search by one of the brothers he
loved best, sitting under his favourite
tree, rapt in ecstasy and surrounded by an
aura of radiant light ; as the discerning
eyes of those who loved them have seen St.
Francis, St. Teresa, and other contemplatives
transfigured and made shining by the intensity of their spiritual life. I need not
point out that the fact that these things are
common form in the lives of the mystics,
does not necessarily discredit them ; though
in any case their interest is less of a mystical
than of a psychological kind.

Not less significant, and to us perhaps
more winning, is that side of Ruysbroeck's
personality which was turned towards the
world of men. In his own person he fulfilled that twofold duty of the deified soul
which he has described to us: the inbreathing of the Love of God, the out-breath-
ing of that same radiant charity towards the
race. " To give and receive, both at once,
is the essence of union," he says; and his
whole career is an illustration of these
words. He took his life from the Tran-

scendent; he was a focus of distribution, which gave out that joyous life again to other souls. His retreat at Groenendael, his ecstasies of composition, never kept him from those who wanted his help and advice. In his highest ascents towards Divine Love, the rich complexities of human love went with him. Other men always meant much to Ruysbroeck. He had a genius for friendship, and gave himself without stint to his friends; and those who knew him said that none ever went to him for consolation without returning with gladness in their hearts. There are many tales in the *Vita* of his power over and intuitive understanding of other minds; of conversions effected, motives unveiled and clouds dispelled. His great friend, Gerard Naghel, the Carthusian prior—at whose desire he wrote one of the most beautiful of his shorter works, *The Book of Supreme Truth*— has left a vivid little account of the impression which his personality created : " his peaceful and joyful countenance, his humble good-humoured speech." Ruysbroeck spent three days in Gerard's monastery, in order to explain some difficult passages in his writings, " and these days were too short, for no one could speak to him or see him without being the better for it."

By this we may put the description of Pomerius, founded upon the reminiscences of Ruysbroeck's surviving friends. "The grace of God shone in his face; and also in his modest speech, his kindly deeds, his humble manners, and in the way that every action of his life exhibited uprightness and radiant purity. He lived soberly, neglected his dress, and was patient in all things and with all people."

Plainly the great contemplative who had seemed in Brussels a 'negligible man,' kept to the end a great simplicity of aspect; closely approximating to his own ideal of the 'really humble man, without any pose or pretence,' as described in *The Spiritual Marriage*. That profound self-immersion in God which was the source of his power, manifested itself in daily life under the least impressive forms; ever seeking embodiment in little concrete acts of love and service, "ministering, in the world without, to all who need, in love and mercy."[1] We see him in his Franciscan love of living things, his deep sense of kinship with all the little children of God, 'going to the help of the animals in all their needs'; thrown into a torment of distress by the brothers who suggested to him that during a hard winter the little birds of the forest might die, and at once making generous and successful arrangements for their entertainment. We see him 'giving Mary and Martha *rendez-vous* in his heart';

[1] *The Twelve Béguines*, cap. vii.

working in the garden of the community, trying hard to be useful, wheeling barrow-loads of manure, and emerging from profound meditation on the Infinite to pull up young vegetables under the impression that they were weeds. He made, in fact, valiant efforts to achieve that perfect synthesis of action and contemplation 'ever abiding in the simplicity of the Spirit, and perpetually flowing forth in abundant acts of love towards heaven and earth,' which he regarded as the proper goal of human growth—efforts constantly thwarted by his own growing concentration on the Transcendent, the ease and frequency with which his consciousness now withdrew from the world of the senses to immerse itself in Spiritual Reality. In theory there was for him no cleavage between the two: Being and Becoming, the Temporal and the Eternal, were but two moods within the mind of God, and in the superessential life of perfect union these completing opposites should merge in one.

A life which shall find place for the activities of the lover, the servant, and the apostle, is the goal towards which the great mystics seem to move. We have seen how the homely life of the priory gave to Ruysbroeck the opportunity of service, how the silence of the forest fostered and supported his secret life of love. As the years passed, the third side of his nature, the apostolic passion which had found during his long Brussels period ample scope for its activities, once more came into prominence. He was sought out by numbers of would-be disciples, not only from Belgium itself, but from Holland, Germany and France; and became a fountainhead of new life, the father of many spiritual children. The tradition which places among these disciples the great Dominican mystic Tauler is probably false; though many passages in Tauler's later sermons suggest that he was strongly influenced by Ruysbroeck's works, which had already attained a wide circulation. But Gerard Groot, afterwards the founder of the Brothers of the Common Life, and spiritual ancestor of Thomas à Kempis, went to Groenendael shortly after his conversion in 1374, that he might there learn the rudiments of a sane and robust spirituality. Ruysbroeck received him with a special joy, recognising in him at first sight a peculiar aptitude for the things of the Spirit. A deep friendship grew up between the old mystic and the young and vigorous convert. Gerard stayed often at the priory, and corresponded regularly with Ruysbroeck; whose influence it was which conditioned his subsequent career as a preacher, and as founder of a congregation as simple and unconventional in its first beginnings, as fruitful in its later developments, as that of Groenendael itself.

The penetrating remarks upon human character scattered through his works, and the anecdotes of his dealings with disciples and penitents preserved by Pomerius, suggest that Ruysbroeck, though he might not always recognise the distinction between the weeds and vegetables of the garden, was seldom at fault in his judgment of men. An instinctive knowledge of the human heart, an unerring eye for insincerity, egotism, self-deception, is a power which nearly all the great contemplatives possess, and often employed with disconcerting effect. I need refer only to the caustic analysis of the 'false contemplative' contained in *The Cloud of Unknowing*, and the amusing sketches of spiritual self-importance in St. Teresa's letters and life. The little tale, so often repeated, of the somewhat self-conscious priests who came from Paris to consult Ruysbroeck on the state of their souls, and received from him only the blunt observation — apparently so careless, yet really plumbing human nature to its deeps — "You are as holy as you wish to be," shows him possessed of this same power of stripping off the husks of unreality and penetrating at once to the fundamental facts of the soul's life: the purity and direction of its will and love.

The life-giving life of union, once man has grown up to it, clarifies, illuminates, raises to a higher term, all aspects of the self : intelligence, no less than love and will. That self is now harmonised about its true centre, and finding ' God in all creatures and all creatures in God ' finds them in their reality. So it is that Ruysbroeck's long life of growth, his long education in love, bringing him to that which he calls the ' God-seeing' stage, brings him to a point in which he finds everywhere Reality : in those rhythmic seasonal changes of the forest life which have inspired his wonderful doctrine of the perpetual rebirth and re-budding of the soul ; in the hearts of men—though often there deep buried—above all, in the mysteries of the Christian faith. Speaking with an unequalled authority and intimacy of those supersensuous regions, those mysterious contacts of love which lie beyond and above all thought, he is yet firmly rooted in the concrete ; for he has reconciled in his own experience the paradox of a Transcendent yet Immanent God. There is no break in the life-process which begins with the little country boy running away from home in quest of some vaguely felt object of desire, some ' better land,' and which ends with the triumphant passing over of the soul of the great contemplative to the perfect fruition of Eternal Love.

Ruysbroeck died at Groenendael on December 2, 1381. He was eighty-eight years old; feeble in body, nearly blind, yet keeping to the last his clear spiritual vision, his vigour and eagerness of soul. His death, says Pomerius, speaking on the authority of those who had seen it, was full of peaceful joy, of gaiety of heart; not the falling asleep of the tired servant, but the leap to more abundant life of the vigorous child of the Infinite, at last set free. With an immense gladness he went out from that time-world which, in his own image, is 'the shadow of God,' to "those high mountains of the land of promise where no shadow is, but only the Sun." One of the greatest of Christian seers, one of the most manly and human of the mystics, it is yet as a lover, in the noblest and most vital sense of the word, that his personality lives for us. From first to last, under all its external accidents, we may trace in his life the activity—first instinctive, and only gradually understood—of that 'unconquerable love,' ardent, industrious, at last utterly surrendered, which he describes in the wonderful tenth chapter of *The Sparkling Stone*, as the unique power which effects the soul's union with God. "For no man understandeth what love is in itself, but such are its workings: which giveth more than one can take, and asketh more than one can pay." That love it was which came out from the Infinite, as a tendency, an instinct endowed with liberty and life, and passed across the stage of history, manifested under humblest inconspicuous forms, but ever growing in passion and power; till at last, achieving the full stature of the children of God, it returned to its Source and Origin again. When we speak of the mysticism of Ruysbroeck, it is of this that we should think: of this growing spirit, this ardent, unconquerable, creative thing. A veritable part of our own order, therein it was transmuted from unreal to real existence; putting on Divine Humanity, and attaining the goal of all life in the interests of the race.

CHAPTER II

HIS WORKS

In all that I have understood, felt, or written, I submit myself to the judgment of the saints and of Holy Church, for I would live and die Christ's servant in Christian Faith.
THE BOOK OF SUPREME TRUTH.

BEFORE discussing Ruysbroeck's view of the spiritual world, his doctrine of the soul's development, perhaps it will be well to consider the traditional names, general character, and contents of his admittedly authentic works. Only a few of these works can be dated with precision; for recent criticism has shown that the so-called chronological list given by Pomerius [1] cannot be accepted. As to several of them, we cannot tell whether they were composed at Brussels or at Groenendael, at the beginning, middle or end of his mystical life. All were written in the Flemish vernacular of his own day—or, strictly speaking, in the dialect of Brabant—for they were practical books composed for a practical object, not

[1] *Vita*, cap. xv.

academic treatises on mystical theology. Founded on experience, they deal with and incite to experience; and were addressed to all who felt within themselves the stirrings of a special grace, the call of a superhuman love, irrespective of education or position—to hermits, priests, nuns, and ardent souls still in the world who were trying to live the one real life—not merely to learned professors trying to elucidate the doctrines of that life. Ruysbroeck therefore belongs to that considerable group of mystical writers whose gift to the history of literature is only less important than their gift to the history of the spiritual world; since they have helped to break down the barrier between the written and the spoken word.

At the moment in which poetry first forsakes the 'literary' language and uses the people's speech, we nearly always find a mystic thus trying to tell his message to the race. His enthusiasm it is which is equal to the task of subduing a new medium to the purposes of art. Thus at the very beginning of Italian poetry we find St. Francis of Assisi singing in the popular tongue his great Canticle of the Sun, and soon after him come the sublime lyrics of Jacopone da Todì. Thus German literature owes much to Mechthild of Magdeburg, and English to Richard Rolle—both forsaking Latin for the common speech of their day.

Thus in India the poet Kabir, obedient to the same impulse, sings in Hindi rather than in Sanscrit his beautiful songs of Divine Love.

In Ruysbroeck, as in these others, a strong poetic inspiration mingled with and sometimes controlled the purely mystical side of his genius. Often his love and enthusiasm break out and express themselves, sometimes in rough, irregular verse, sometimes in rhymed and rhythmic prose: a kind of wild spontaneous chant, which may be related to the 'ghostly song' that 'boiled up' within the heart of Richard Rolle. It is well-known that automatic composition—and we have seen that the evidence of those who knew him suggests the presence of an automatic element in Ruysbroeck's creative methods—tends to assume a rhythmic character; being indeed closely related to that strange chanted speech in which religious excitement frequently expresses itself. Released from the control of the surface-intellect, the deeper mind which is involved in these mysterious processes tends to present its intuitions and concepts in measured waves of words; which sometimes, as in Rolle's 'ghostly song' and perhaps too in Ruysbroeck's 'Song of Joy,' are actually given a musical form. In such rhythm the mystic seems to catch something of the cadences of that far-off music of which he is writing, and to receive and transmit a message which exceeds the possibilities of speech. Ruysbroeck was no expert poet. Often his verse is bad; halting in cadence, violent and uncouth in imagery, like the stammering utterance of one possessed. But its presence and quality, its mingled simplicity and violence, assure us of the strong excitement that fulfilled him, and tend to corroborate the account of his mental processes which we have deduced from the statements in Pomerius' *Life*.

Eleven admittedly authentic books and tracts survive in numerous MS. collections,[1] and from these come all that we know of his vision and teaching. *The Twelve Virtues*, and the two Canticles often attributed to him, are probably spurious; and the tracts against the Brethren of the Free Spirit, which are known to have been written during his Brussels period, have all disappeared. I give here a short account of the authentic works, their names and general contents; putting first in order those of unknown date, some of which may possibly have been composed before the foundation of Groenendael. In each case the first title is a translation of that used in the best Flemish texts; the second,

[1] De Vreese has identified 160 Flemish and 46 Latin MSS. of Ruysbroeck.

that employed in the great Latin version of Surius. Ruysbroeck himself never gave any titles to his writings.

1. THE SPIRITUAL TABERNACLE (called by Surius *In Tabernaculum Mosis*).—The longest, most fantastic, and, in spite of some fine passages, the least interesting of Ruysbroeck's works. Probably founded upon the *De Arca Mystica* of Hugh of St. Victor, this is an elaborate allegory, thoroughly mediæval in type, in which the Tabernacle of the Israelites becomes a figure of the spiritual life; the details of its construction, furniture and ritual being given a symbolic significance, in accordance with the methods of interpretation popular at the time. In this book, and perhaps in the astronomical treatise appended to *The Twelve Béguines* (No. 11), I believe that we have the only surviving works of Ruysbroeck's first period; when he had not yet 'transcended images,' but was at that point in his mystical development in which the young contemplative loves to discern symbolic meanings in all visible things.

2. THE TWELVE POINTS OF TRUE FAITH (*De Fide et Judicio*). — This little tract is in form a gloss upon the Nicene Creed; in fact, a characteristically Ruysbroeckian confession of faith. Without ever over-passing the boundaries of Catholic doctrine, Ruysbroeck is here able to turn all

its imagery to the purposes of his own vision of truth.

3. THE BOOK OF THE FOUR TEMPTATIONS (*De Quatuor Tentationibus*). — The Four Temptations are four manifestations of the higher egotism specially dangerous to souls entering on the contemplative life : first, the love of ease and comfort, as much in things spiritual as in things material; secondly, the tendency to pose as the possessor of special illumination, with other and like forms of spiritual pretence ; thirdly, intellectual pride, which seeks to understand unfathomable mysteries and attain to the vision of God by the reason alone ; fourthly, —most dangerous of all—that false 'liberty of spirit' which was the mark of the heretical mystic sects. This book too may well have been written before the retreat to Groenendael.

4. THE BOOK OF THE KINGDOM OF GOD'S LOVERS (*Regnum Deum Amantium*).—This and the following work, *The Adornment of the Spiritual Marriage*, contain Ruysbroeck's fullest and most orderly descriptions of the mystical life-process. The 'Kingdom' which God's lovers may inherit is the actual life of God, infused into the soul and deifying it. This essential life reveals itself under five modes : in the sense world, in the soul's nature, in the witness of Scripture, in the life of grace or 'glory,'

and in the Superessential Kingdom of the
Divine Unity. By the threefold way of
the Active, Contemplative, and Superessential Life, here described as the steady and
orderly appropriation of the Seven Gifts
of the Holy Spirit, the spirit of man may
enter into its inheritance and attain at last
to the perfect fruition of God. To the Active
Life belong the gifts of Holy Fear, Godliness,
and Knowledge; to the Contemplative those
of Strength and Counsel; to the Superessential those of Intelligence and Wisdom.
The Kingdom of God's Lovers was traditionally regarded as Ruysbroeck's earliest
work. It was more probably written during
the early years at Groenendael. Much of
it, like *The Twelve Béguines*, is in poetical
form. This was the book which, falling into
the hands of Gerard Naghel, made him seek
Ruysbroeck's acquaintance, in order that
he might ask for an explanation of several
profound and difficult passages.

5. THE ADORNMENT OF THE SPIRITUAL
MARRIAGE (*De Ornatu Spiritalium Nuptiarum*).—This is the best known and most
methodical of Ruysbroeck's works. In form
a threefold commentary upon the text,
" Behold, the bridegroom cometh; go ye
out to meet him," it is divided into three
books, tracing out in great detail, and with
marvellous psychological insight, those three
stages of Active, Contemplative and Super-

HIS WORKS

essential Life, which appear again and again in his writings. Paying due attention to the aberrations of the quietists, he exhibits—with an intimacy which surely reflects his own personal experience of the Way—the conditions under which selves in each stage of development may see, encounter, and at last unite with, the Divine Bridegroom of the soul. A German translation of several of its chapters, preserved in MS. at Munich, states that Ruysbroeck sent this book to the Friends of God in 1350. In this case it belongs to the years immediately preceding or succeeding his retreat.

We now come to the works which were certainly composed at Groenendael, though probably some of those already enumerated also belong to the last thirty years of Ruysbroeck's life. First come the three treatises apparently written for Margaret van Meerbeke, a choir nun of the Convent of Poor Clares at Brussels; who seems to have been to him what St. Clare was to St. Francis, Elizabeth Stägel to Suso, Margaret Kirkby to Richard Rolle—first a spiritual daughter, then a valued and sympathetic friend.

6. THE MIRROR OF ETERNAL SALVATION or BOOK OF THE BLESSED SACRAMENT (*Speculum Æternæ Salutis*). — This, the first of the three, was written in 1359. It is addressed to one who is evidently a beginner in the spiritual life, as she is yet a novice in

her religious community; but whom Ruysbroeck looks upon as specially 'called, elect and loved.' In simplest language, often of extreme beauty, he puts before her the magnitude of the vocation she has accepted, the dangers she will encounter, and the great source from which she must draw her strength : the sacramental dispensation of the Church. In a series of magnificent chapters, he celebrates the mystical doctrine of the Eucharist, the feeding of the evergrowing soul on the substance of God; following this by a digression, full of shrewd observation, on the different types of believers who come to communion. We see them through his eyes : the religious sentimentalists, 'who are generally women and only very seldom men'; the sturdy normal Christian, who does his best to struggle against sin; the humble and devout lover of God; the churchy hypocrite, who behaves with great reverence at Mass and then goes home and scolds the servants; the heretical mystic full of spiritual pride; the easy-going worldling, who sins and repents with equal facility. The book ends with a superb description of the goal towards which the young contemplative is set : the 'life-giving life' of perfect union with God in which that 'higher life' latent in every soul at last attains to maturity.

7. THE SEVEN CLOISTERS (*De Septem*

Custodiis).—This was written before 1363, and preserves its address to 'The Holy Nun, Dame Margaret van Meerbeke, Cantor of the Monastery of St. Clare at Brussels.' The novice of the 'Mirror' is now a professed religious; and her director instructs her upon the attitude of mind which she should bring to the routine duties of a nun's day, the opportunity they offer for the enriching and perfecting of love and humility. He describes the education of the human spirit up to that high point of consciousness where it knows itself established 'between Eternity and Time': one of the fundamental thoughts of Flemish and German mysticism. This education admits her successively into the seven cloisters which kept St. Clare, Foundress of the Order, unspotted from the world. The first is the physical enclosure of the convent walls; the next the moral and volitional limitation of self-control. The third is 'the open door of the love of Christ,' which crowns man's affective powers, and leads to the fourth—total dedication of the will. The fifth and sixth represent the two great forms of the Contemplative Life as conceived by Ruysbroeck: the ecstatic and the deiform. The seventh admits to Abyss of Being itself: that 'dim silence' at the heart of which, as in the Seventh Habitation of St. Teresa's 'Interior Castle,' he will find himself alone with God. There the mystic union is consummated, and the Divine activity takes the place of the separate activity of man, in "a simple beatitude which transcends all sanctity and the practice of virtue, an Eternal Fruition which satisfies all hunger and thirst, all love and all craving, for God." Finally, he returns to the Active Life; and ends with a practical chapter on clothes, and a charming instruction, full of deep poetry, on the evening meditation which should close the day.

8. THE SEVEN DEGREES OF THE LADDER OF LOVE (*De Septem Gradibus Amoris*).—This book, which was written before 1372, is believed by the Benedictines of Wisques, the latest and most learned of Ruysbroeck's editors, to complete the trilogy of works addressed to Dame Margaret van Meerbeke. It traces the soul's ascent to the height of Divine love by way of the charactcristic virtues of asceticism, under the well-known mediæval image of the 'ladder of perfection' or 'stairway of love'—a metaphor, originating in Jacob's Dream, which had already served St. Benedict, Richard of St. Victor, St. Bonaventura and many others as a useful diagram of the mystic way. Originality of form, however, is the last thing we should look for in Ruysbroeck's works. He pours his strange wine into any vessel that comes to hand. As often his most sublime or amazing utterances origin-

ate in commentaries upon some familiar text, or the deepest truths are hidden under the most grotesque similitudes; so this well-worn metaphor gives him the opportunity for some of his finest descriptions of the soul's movement to that transmutation in which all ardent spirits 'become as live coals in the fire of Infinite Love.' This book, in which the influence of St. Bernard is strongly marked, contains some beautiful passages on the mystic life considered as a 'heavenly song' of faithfulness and love, which "Christ our Cantor and our Choragus has sung from the beginning of things," and which every Christian soul must learn.

9. THE BOOK OF THE SPARKLING STONE (*De Calculo, sive de Perfectione Filiorum Dei*).—This priceless work is said to have been written by Ruysbroeck at the request of a hermit, who wished for further light on the high matters of which it treats. It contains the finest flower of his thought, and shows perhaps more clearly than any other of his writings the mark of direct inspiration. Here again the scaffolding on which he builds is almost as old as Christian mysticism itself: that three-fold division of men into the 'faithful servants, secret friends, and hidden sons' of God, which descended through the centuries from Clement of Alexandria. But the tower which he raises with its help ascends to heights unreached by

any other writer: to the point at which man is given the supreme gift of the Sparkling Stone, or Nature of Christ, the goal of human transcendence. I regard the ninth and tenth chapters of *The Sparkling Stone*— 'How we may become Hidden Sons of God and live the Contemplative Life,' and 'How we, though one with God, must eternally remain other than Him' — as the high-water mark of mystical literature. Nowhere else do we find such a marvellous combination of wide and soaring vision with the most delicate and intimate psychological analysis. The old mystic, sitting under his friendly tree, seems here to be gazing at and reporting to us the final secrets of that eternal world, where "the Incomprehensible Light enfolds and penetrates us, as the air is penetrated by the light of the sun." There he tastes and apprehends, in 'an unfathomable seeing and beholding,' the inbreathing and the outbreathing of the Love of God—that double movement which controls the universe; yet knows, along with this great cosmic vision, that intimate and searching communion in which "the Beloved and the Lover are immersed wholly in love, and each is all to the other in possession and in rest."

10. THE BOOK OF SUPREME TRUTH (called in some collections *The Book of Retractations*, and by Surius, *Samuel*.)—This is the tract

written by Ruysbroeck, at the request of Gerard Naghel, to explain certain obscure passages in *The Book of the Kingdom of God's Lovers*. In it he is specially concerned to make clear the vital distinction between his doctrine of the soul's union with God—a union in which the primal distinction between Creator and created is never overpassed—and the pantheistic doctrine of complete absorption in Him, with cessation of all effort and striving, preached by the heretical sects whose initiates claim to 'be God.' By the time that this book was written, careless readers had already charged Ruysbroeck with these pantheist tendencies which he abhorred and condemned; and here he sets out his defence. He discusses also the three degrees of union with God which correspond to the 'three lives' of the growing soul: union by means of sacraments and good deeds; union achieved in contemplative prayer 'without means,' where the soul learns its double vocation of action and fruition; and the highest union of all, where the spirit which has swung pendulumlike between the temporal and eternal worlds, achieves its equilibrium and dwells wholly in God, 'drunk with love, and sunk in the Dark Light.'

11. THE TWELVE BÉGUINES (*De Vera Contemplatione*).—This is a long, composite book of eighty-four chapters, which apparently

consists of at least three distinct treatises
of different dates. The first, *The Twelve
Béguines*, which ends with chapter xvi.,
contains the longest consecutive example of
Ruysbroeck's poetic method; its first eight
chapters being written in irregular rhymed
verse. It is believed to be one of his last
compositions. Its doctrine differs little from
that already set forth in his earlier works;
though nowhere, perhaps, is the development of the spiritual consciousness described with greater subtlety. The soul's
communion with and feeding on the Divine
Nature in the Eucharist and in contemplative prayer; its acquirement of the art
of introversion; the Way of Contemplation
with its four modes, paralleled by the Way of
Love with its four modes; these lead up
to the perfect union of the spirit with God
" in one love and one fruition with Him,
fulfilled in everlasting bliss." The seven-
teenth chapter begins a new treatise, with a
description of the Active Life on Ruysbroeck's usual lines; and at the thirtieth
there is again a complete change of subject,
introducing a mystical and symbolic interpretation of the science of astronomy. This
section, so unlike his later writings, somewhat resembles *The Spiritual Tabernacle*,
and may perhaps be a work of the same
period. A collection of Meditations upon
the Passion of Christ, arranged according

HIS WORKS

to the Seven Hours of the Roman Breviary (capp. lxxiii. to end), completes the book; and also the tale of Ruysbroeck's authentic works. A critical list of the reprints and translations in which these may best be studied will be found in the Bibliographical Note.

CHAPTER III

HIS DOCTRINE OF GOD

My words are strange; but those who love will understand.   THE MIRROR OF ETERNAL SALVATION.

MYSTICAL writers are of two kinds. One kind, of which St. Teresa is perhaps the supreme type, deals almost wholly with the personal and interior experiences of the soul in the states of contemplation, and the psychological rules governing those states; above all, with the emotional reactions of the self to the impact of the Divine. This kind of mystic — whom William James accused, with some reason, of turning the soul's relation with God into a ' duet '—makes little attempt to describe the ultimate Object of the self's love and desire, the great movements of the spiritual world; for such description, the formulæ of existing theology are felt to be enough. Visions of Christ, experiences of the Blessed Trinity—these are sufficient names for the personal and impersonal aspects of that Reality with which the contemplative seeks to unite. But the

HIS DOCTRINE OF GOD

other kind of mystic—though possibly and indeed usually as orthodox in his beliefs, as ardent in his love—cannot, on the one hand, remain within the circle of these subjective and personal conceptions, and, on the other, content himself with the label which tradition has affixed to the Thing that he has known. He may not reject the label, but neither does he confuse it with the Thing. He has the wide vision, the metaphysical passion of the philosopher and the poet ; and in his work he is ever pressing towards more exact description, more suggestive and evocative speech. The symbols which come most naturally to him are usually derived from the ideas of space and of wonder; not from those of human intimacy and love. In him the intellect is active as well as the heart ; sometimes, more active. Plotinus is an extreme example of mysticism of this type.

The greatest mystics, however, whether in the East or in the West, are possessed of a vision and experience of God so deep and rich that it embraces at once the infinite and the intimate aspects of Reality ; illuminating those religious concepts which are, as it were, an artistic reconstruction of the Transcendent, and at the same time having contact with that vast region above and beyond reason whence come the fragmentary intimations of Reality crystallised in the formulæ of faith. For them, as for St. Augustine, God is both near and far; and the paradox of transcendent-immanent Reality is a self-evident if an inexpressible truth. They swing between hushed adoration and closest communion, between the divine ignorance of the intellect lifted up into God and the divine certitude of the heart in which He dwells; and give us by turns a subjective and psychological, an objective and metaphysical, reading of spiritual experience. Ruysbroeck is a mystic of this type. The span of his universe can include — indeed demand — both the concept of that Abyss of Pure Being where all distinctions are transcended, and the soul is immersed in the ' dark light ' of the One, and the distinctively Christian and incarnational experience of loving communion with and through the Person of Christ. For him the ladder of contemplation is firmly planted in the bed-rock of human character —goes the whole way from the heart of man to the Essence of God—and every stage of it has importance for the eager and ascending soul. Hence, when he seems to rush out to the farthest limits of the cosmos, he still remains within the circle of Catholic ideas; and is at once ethical and metaphysical, intensely sacramental and intensely transcendental too.

Nor is this result obtained—as it sometimes

seems to be, for instance, in such a visionary as Angela of Foligno—by a mere heaping up of the various and inconsistent emotional reactions of the self. There is a fundamental orderliness in the Ruysbroeckian universe which, though it may be difficult to understand, and often impossible for him to express without resort to paradox, yet reveals itself to careful analysis. He tries hard to describe, or at least suggest, it to us, because he is a mystic of an apostolic type. Even where he is dealing with the soul's most ineffable experiences and seems to hover over that Abyss which is 'beyond Reason,' stammering and breaking into wild poetry in the desperate attempt to seize the unseizable truth, he is ever intent on telling us how these things may be actualised, this attitude attained by other men. The note is never, as with many subjective visionaries, "*I* have seen," but always "*We* shall or may see."

Now such an objective mystic as this, who is not content with retailing his private experiences and ecstasies, but accepts the great vocation of revealer of Reality, is called upon to do certain things. He must give us, not merely a static picture of Eternity, but also a dynamic 'reading of life'; and of a life more extended than that which the moralist, or even the philosopher, offers to interpret. He must not only tell

us what he thinks about the universe, and
in particular that ultimate Spiritual Reality
which all mysticism discerns within or
beyond the flux. He must also tell us what
he thinks of man, that living, moving, fluid
spirit-thing: his reactions to this universe
and this Reality, the satisfaction which it
offers to his thought, will and love, the
obligations laid upon him in respect of it.
We, on our part, must try to understand what
he tells us of these things; for he is, as it
were, an organ developed by the race for
this purpose — a tentacle pushed out towards the Infinite, to make, in our name and
in our interest, fresh contacts with Reality.
He performs for us some of the functions
of the artist extending our universe, the
pioneer cutting our path, the hunter winning
food for our souls.

The clue to the universe of such a mystic
will always be the vision or idea which he
has of the Nature of God; and there we
must begin, if we would find our way through
the tangle of his thought. From this
Centre all else branches out, and to this
all else must conform, if it is to have for him
realness and life; for truth, as Aquinas
teaches, is simply the reality of things as
they are in God. We begin, then, our exploration of Ruysbroeck's doctrine by trying
to discover the character of his vision of the
Divine Nature, and man's relation with it.

That vision is so wide, deep and searching, that only by resort to the language of opposites, by perpetual alternations of spatial and personal, metaphysical and passionate speech, is he able to communicate it to us. His fortunate and profound acquaintance with the science of theology—his contact through it with the formulæ of Christian Platonism—has given him the framework on which he stretches out his wonderful and living picture of the Infinite. This picture is personal to himself, the fruit of a direct and vivid inspiration ; not so the terms by which it is communicated. These for the most part are the common property of Christian theology ; though here used with a consummate skill, often with an apparent originality. Especially from St. Augustine, Dionysius the Areopagite, Richard of St. Victor, St. Bernard and the more orthodox utterances of his own immediate predecessor, Meister Eckhart—sometimes too from his contemporaries, Suso and Tauler—has he taken the intellectual concepts, the highly-charged poetic metaphors, in which his perceptions are enshrined. So close does he keep to these masters, so frequent are his borrowings, that almost every page of his writings might be glossed from their works. It is one of the most astonishing features of the celebrated and astonishing essay of M. Maeterlinck that, bent on vindicating the inspiration of his ' simple and ignorant monk,' he entirely fails to observe the traditional character of the formulæ which express it. No student of the mystics will deny the abundant inspiration by which Ruysbroeck was possessed; but this inspiration is spiritual, not intellectual. The truth was told to him in the tongue of angels, and he did his best to translate it into the tongue of the Church; perpetually reminding us, as he did so, how great was the difference between vision and description, how clumsy and inadequate those concepts and images wherewith the artist-seer tried to tell his love.

This distinction, which the reader of Ruysbroeck should never forget, is of primary importance in connection with his treatment of the Nature of God; where the disparity between the thing known and the thing said is inevitably at a maximum. The high nature of the Godhead, he says, in a string of suggestive and paradoxical images, to which St. Paul, Dionysius and Eckhart have all contributed, is, in itself, " Simplicity and One-foldness; inaccessible height and fathomless deep; incomprehensible breadth and eternal length; a dim silence, and a wild desert "—oblique, suggestive, musical language which enchants rather than informs the soul; opens the door to experience, but does not convey any accurate knowledge of the Imageless Truth. " Now we may experience many wonders in that fathomless Godhead ; but although, because of the coarseness of the human intellect, when we would describe such things outwardly, we must use images, in truth that which is inwardly perceived and beheld is nought else but a Fathomless and Unconditioned Good." [1]

Yet this primal Reality, this ultimately indivisible One, has for human consciousness a two-fold character ; and though for the intuition of the mystic its fruition is a synthetic experience, it must in thought be analysed if it is ever to be grasped. God, as known by man, exhibits in its perfection the dual property of Love ; on the one hand active, generative, creative ; on the other hand a still and ineffable possession or *Fruition*—one of the master-words of Ruysbroeck's thought. He is, then, the Absolute One, in whom the antithesis of Eternity and Time, of Being and Becoming, is resolved ; both static and dynamic, transcendent and immanent, impersonal and personal, undifferentiated and differentiated ; Eternal Rest and Eternal Work, the Unmoved Mover, yet Movement itself. "Although in our way of seeing we give God many names, His nature is One."

He transcends the storm of succession, yet

[1] *The Spiritual Marriage*, lib. ii. cap. xxxvii.

is the inspiring spirit of the flux. According to His fruitful nature, " He works without ceasing, for He is Pure Act "—a reminiscence of Aristotle which seems strange upon the lips of the 'ignorant monk.' He is the omnipotent and ever-active Creator of all things; 'an immeasurable Flame of Love' perpetually breathing forth His energetic Life in new births of being and new floods of grace, and drawing in again all creatures to Himself. Yet this statement defines, not His being, but one manifestation of His being. When the soul pierces beyond this 'fruitful' nature to His simple essence—and 'simple' is here and throughout to be understood in its primal meaning of 'synthetic'—He is that absolute and abiding Reality which seems to man Eternal Rest, the 'Deep Quiet of the Godhead,' the 'Abyss,' the 'Dim Silence'; and which we can taste indeed but never know. There, 'all lovers lose themselves' in the consummation of that experience at which our fragmentary intuitions hint.

The active and fertile aspect of the Divine Nature is manifested in differentiation : for Ruysbroeck the Catholic, in the Trinity of Persons, as defined by Christian theology. The static and absolute aspect is the 'calm and glorious Unity of the Godhead' which he finds beyond and within the Trinity, "the fathomless Abyss that *is* the Being of God,"

HIS DOCTRINE OF GOD

—an idea, familiar to Indian mysticism and implicit in Christian Neoplatonism, which governed all Meister Eckhart's speculations upon the Divine Nature. There is, says Ruysbroeck in one of his most Eckhartian passages, "a distinction and differentiation, according to our reason, between God and the Godhead, between action and rest. The fruitful nature of the Persons, of whom is the Trinity in Unity and Unity in Trinity, ever worketh in a living differentiation. But the Simple Being of God, according to the nature thereof, is an Eternal Rest of God and of all created things."[1]

In differentiating the three great aspects of the Divine Life, as known by the love and thought of man, Ruysbroeck keeps close to formal theology; though investing its academic language with new and deep significance, and constantly reminding us that such language, even at its best, can never get beyond the region of image and similitude or provide more than an imperfect reflection of the One who is 'neither This nor That.' On his lips, credal definitions are perpetually passing over from the arid region of theological argument to the fruitful one of spiritual experience. There they become songs, as 'new' as the song heard by the Apocalyptist; real channels of light, which show the mind things that it never

[1] *The Twelve Béguines*, cap. xiv.

guessed before. For the 're-born' man they have a fresh and immortal meaning; because that 'river of grace,' of which he perpetually speaks as pouring into the heart opened towards the Infinite, transfigures and irradiates them. Thus the illuminated mind knows in the Father, not a confusingly anthropomorphic metaphor, but the uniquely vital Source and unconditioned Origin of all things "in whom our life and being is begun." He is the "Strength and Power, Creator, Mover, Keeper, Beginning and End, Cause and Existence of all creatures."[1] Further, the intuition of the mystic discerns in the Son the Eternal Word and fathomless Wisdom and Truth perpetually generated of the Father, shining forth in the world of conditions: the Pattern or Archetype of creation and of life, the image of God which the universe reflects back before the face of the Absolute, the Eternal Rule incarnate in Christ. And this same 'light wherein we see God' also shows to the enlightened mind the veritable character of the Holy Spirit; the Incomprehensible Love and Generosity of the Divine Nature, which emanates in an eternal procession from the mutual contemplation of Father and Son, "for these two Persons are always hungry for love." The Holy Spirit is the source of the Divine vitality immanent in the uni-

[1] *The Spiritual Marriage*, lib. ii. cap. xxxvii.

verse. It is an outflowing torrent of Good
which streams through all heavenly spirits;
it is a Flame of Fire that consumes all in
the One; it is also the Spark of transcendence latent in man's soul. The Spirit
is the personal, Grace the impersonal, side
of that energetic Love which enfolds and
penetrates all life; and "all this may be
perceived and beheld, inseparable and
without division, in the Simple Nature of
the Godhead." [1]

The relations which form the character
of these Three Persons exist in an eternal
distinction for that world of conditions
wherein the human soul is immersed, and
where things happen 'in some wise.' There,
from the embrace of the Father and Son
and the outflowing of the Spirit in 'waves
of endless love,' all created things are born;
and God, by His grace and His death, re-
creates them, and adorns them with love
and goodness, and draws them back to
their source. This is the circling course of
the Divine life-process 'from goodness,
through goodness, to goodness,' described by
Dionysius the Areopagite. But beyond and
above this plane of Divine differentiation
is the superessential world, transcending all
conditions, inaccessible to thought — " the
measureless solitude of the Godhead, where
God possesses Himself in joy." This is the

[1] *Op. cit., ibid.*

ultimate world of the mystic, discerned by intuition and love "in a simple seeing, beyond reason and without consideration." There, within the 'Eternal Now,' without either before or after, released from the storm of succession, things happen indeed, 'yet in no wise.' There, "we can speak no more of Father, Son and Holy Spirit, nor of any creature; but only of one Being, which is the very substance of the Divine Persons. There were we all one before our creation; for this is our *superessence*. . . . There the Godhead is, in simple essence, without activity; Eternal Rest, Unconditioned Dark, the Nameless Being, the Superessence of all created things, and the simple and infinite Bliss of God and of all Saints." [1]

Ruysbroeck here brings us to the position of Dante in the last canto of the *Paradiso*, when, transcending those partial apprehensions of Reality which are figured by the River of Becoming and the Rose of Beatitude, he penetrated to the swift vision of "that Eternal Light which only in Itself abideth"—discerned best by man under the image of the three circles, yet in its 'profound and clear substance' indivisibly One.

"The simple light of this Being is limitless in its immensity, and transcending

[1] *The Seven Degrees of Love*, cap. xiv.

form, includes and embraces the unity of the Divine Persons and the soul with all its faculties; and this to such a point that it envelopes and irradiates *both* the natural tendency of our ground [*i.e.* its dynamic movement to God—the River] and the fruitive adherence of God and all those who are united with Him in this Light [*i.e* Eternal Being—the Rose]. And this is the union of God and the souls that love Him." [1]

[1] *The Kingdom of God's Lovers,* cap. xxix.

CHAPTER IV

HIS DOCTRINE OF MAN

That which was begun by Grace, is accomplished by Grace and Free-will; so that they work mixedly not separately, simultaneously not successively, in each and all of their processes.   St. Bernard.

The concept of the Nature of God which we have traced through its three phases—out from the unchanging One to the active Persons and back to the One again—gives us a clue to Ruysbroeck's idea of the nature and destiny of man. In man, both aspects of Divine Reality, active and fruitive, are or should be reflected; for God is the 'Living Pattern of Creation' who has impressed His image on each soul, and in every adult spirit the character of that image must be brought from the hiddenness and realised. Destined to be wholly real, though yet in the making, there is in man a latent Divine likeness, a 'spark' of the primal fire. Created for union with God, already in Eternity that union is a fact.

"The creature is in Brahma and Brahma

HIS DOCTRINE OF MAN 67

is in the creature; they are ever distinct yet ever united," says the Indian mystic. Were it translated into Christian language, it is probable that this thought—which does *not* involve pantheism—would have been found acceptable by Ruysbroeck; for the interpenetration yet eternal distinction of the human and Divine spirits is the central fact of his universe. Man, he thinks, is already related in a threefold manner to his Infinite Source; for "we have our being in Him as the Father, we contemplate Him as does the Son, we ceaselessly tend to return to Him as does the Spirit."

"The first property of the soul is a *naked being*, devoid of all image. Thereby do we resemble, and are united to, the Father and His nature Divine." This is the 'ground of the soul' perpetually referred to by mystics of the Eckhartian School; the bare, still place to which consciousness retreats in introversion, image of the static and absolute aspect of Reality. "The second property might be called the *higher understanding* of the soul. It is a mirror of light, wherein we receive the Son of God, the Eternal Truth. By this light we are like unto Him; but in the act of receiving, we are one with Him." This is the power of knowing Divine things by intuitive comprehension: man's fragmentary share in the character of the Logos, or Wisdom of

God. "The third property we call the *spark* of the soul. It is the inward and natural tendency of the soul towards its Source; and here do we receive the Holy Spirit, the Charity of God. By this inward tendency we are like the Holy Spirit; but in the act of receiving, we become one spirit and one love with God."[1] Here the Divine image shows itself in its immanent and dynamic aspect, as the 'internal push' which drives Creation back to the Father's heart.

The soul then is, as Julian of Norwich said, "made Trinity, like to the unmade Blessed Trinity." Reciprocally, there is in the Eternal World the uncreated Pattern or Archetype of man—his 'Platonic idea.' Now man must bring from its hiddenness the latent likeness, the germ of Divine humanity that is in him, and develop it until it realises the 'Platonic idea'; achieving thus the implicit truth of his own nature as it exists in the mind of God. This, according to Ruysbroeck, is the whole art and object of the spiritual life; this actualisation of the eternal side of human nature, atrophied in the majority of men—the innate Christliness in virtue of which we have power to become 'Sons' of God.

"Lo! thus are we all one with God in our Eternal Archetype, which is His Wisdom who hath put on the nature of us all. And

[1] *The Mirror of Eternal Salvation*, cap. viii.

although we are already one with Him therein by that putting on of our nature, we must also be like God in grace and virtue, if we would find ourselves one with Him in our Eternal Archetype, which is Himself." [1]

Under the stimulus of Divine Love perpetually beating in on him, feeding perpetually on the substance of God, perpetually renewed and 'reborn' on to ever higher levels through the vivifying contact of reality, man must grow up into the 'superessential life' of complete unity with the Transcendent. There, not only the triune aspect but the dual character of God is reproduced in him, reconciled in a synthesis beyond the span of thought; and he becomes 'deiform'—both active and fruitive, 'ever at work and ever at rest'— at once a denizen of Eternity and of Time. Every aspect of his being—love, intellect and will—is to be invaded and enhanced by the new life-giving life; it shall condition and enrich his correspondences with the sense-world as well as with the world of soul.

Man is not here invited to leave the active life for the contemplative, but to make the active life perfect within the contemplative; carrying up these apparent opposites to a point at which they become one. It is one of Ruysbroeck's characteristics that he, as few others, followed mysticism out to

[1] *The Twelve Béguines,* cap. ix.

this, its last stage; where it issues in a balanced, divine-human life. The energetic Love of God, which flows perpetually forth from the Abyss of Being to the farthest limits of the universe, enlightening and quickening where it goes, and ' turns again home' as a strong tide drawing all things to their Origin, here attains equilibrium; the effort of creation achieves its aim.

Now this aim, this goal, is already realised within God's nature, for there all perfection eternally Is. But to man it is super-nature; to achieve it he must transcend the world of conditions in which he lives according to the flesh, and grow up to fresh levels of life. Under the various images of sonship, marriage, and transmutation, this is the view of human destiny which Ruysbroeck states again and again : the creative evolution of the soul. His insistence on the completeness of the Divine Union to which the soul attains in this final phase, his perpetual resort to the dangerous language of deification in the effort towards describing it, seems at first sight to expose him to the charge of pantheism; and, as a matter of fact, has done so in the past. Yet he is most careful to guard himself at every point against this misinterpretation of his vision of life. In his view, by its growth towards God, personality is not lost, but raised to an ever higher plane. Even in that ecstatic fruition of Eternal Life in which the spirit passes above the state of Union to the state of Unity, and beyond the Persons to the One, the 'eternal otherness' of Creator and created is not overpassed; but, as in the perfect fulfilment of love, utter fusion and clear differentiation mysteriously co-exist. It is, he says, not a mergence but a 'mutual inhabitation.' In his attempts towards the description of this state, he borrows the language of St. Bernard, most orthodox of the mystics; language which goes back to primitive Christian times. The Divine light, love and being, he tells us, penetrates and drenches the surrendered, naked, receptive soul, 'as fire does the iron, as sunlight does the air'; and even as the sunshine and the air, the iron and the fire, so are these two terms distinct yet united. "The iron doth not become fire nor the fire iron; but each retaineth its substance and its nature. So likewise the spirit of man doth not become God, but is God-formed, and knoweth itself breadth and length and height and depth."[1] Again, "this union is *in* God, through grace and our homeward-tending love. Yet even here does the creature feel a distinction and otherness between itself and God in its inward ground"[2] The dualistic relation of lover and beloved,

[1] *The Twelve Béguines*, cap. xiv.
[2] *The Book of Truth*, cap. xi.

though raised to another power and glory, is an eternal one.

I have spoken of Ruysbroeck's concept of God, his closely related concept of man's soul; the threefold diagram of Reality within which these terms are placed, the doctrine of transcendence he deduced therefrom. But such a diagram cannot express to us the rich content, the deeply personal character of his experience and his knowledge. It is no more than a map of the living land he has explored, a formal picture of the Living One whom he has seen without sight. For him the landscape lived and flowered in endless variety of majesty and sweetness; the Person drew near in mysterious communion, and gave to him as food His very life.

All that this meant, and must mean, for our deeper knowledge of Reality and of man's intuitive contacts with the Divine Life, we must find if we can in his doctrine of Love. Love is the ' very self-hood ' of God, says Ruysbroeck in strict Johannine language. His theology is above all the theology of the Holy Spirit, the immanent Divine Energy and Love. It is Love which breaks down the barrier between finite and infinite life. But Love, as he understands it, has little in common with the feeling-state to which many of the female mystics have given that august name. For him, it is hardly an emotional word at all, and never a sentimental one; rather the title of a mighty force, a holy energy that fills the universe—the essential activity of God. Sometimes he describes it under the antique imagery of Light; imagery which is more than a metaphor, and is connected with that veritable consciousness of enhanced radiance, as well in the outer as in the inner world, experienced by the 'illuminated' mystic. Again it is the 'life-giving Life,' hidden in God and the substance of our souls, which the self finds and appropriates; the whole Johannine trilogy brought into play, to express its meaning for heart, intellect and will. This Love, in fact, is the dynamic power which St. Augustine compared with gravitation, 'drawing all things to their own place,' and which Dante saw binding the multiplicity of the universe into one. All Ruysbroeck's images for it turn on the idea of force. It is a raging fire, a storm, a flood. He speaks of it in one great passage as 'playing like lightning' between God and the soul.

Whoever will look at William Blake's great picture of the Creation of Adam, may gain some idea of the terrific yet infinitely compassionate character inherent in this concept of Divine Love: the agony, passion, beauty, sternness, and pity of the primal generating force. This love is eternally giving and taking—it is its very property, says Ruysbroeck, 'ever to give and ever to receive'—pouring its dower of energy into the soul, and drawing out from that soul new vitality, new love, new surrender. 'Hungry love,' 'generous love,' 'stormy love,' he calls it again and again. Streaming out from the heart of Reality, the impersonal aspect of the very Spirit of God, its creative touch evokes in man, once he becomes conscious of it, an answering storm of love. The whole of our human growth within the spiritual order is conditioned by the quality of this response; by the will, the industry, the courage, with which man accepts his part in the Divine give-and-take.

"That measureless Love which is God Himself, dwells in the pure deeps of our spirit, like a burning brazier of coal. And it throws forth brilliant and fiery sparks which stir and enkindle heart and senses, will and desire, and all the powers of the soul, with a fire of love; in a storm, a rage, a measureless fury of love. These be the weapons with which we fight against the terrible and immense Love of God, who would consume all loving spirits and swallow them in Himself. Love arms us with its own gifts, and clarifies our reason, and commands, counsels and advises us to oppose Him, to fight against Him, and to maintain against Him our right to love, so long as we may." [1] In the spiritual realm, giving and receiving are one act, for God is an 'ocean that ebbs and flows'; and it is only by opposing love to love, by self-donation to His mysterious movements, that the soul appropriates new force, invigorating and fertilising it afresh. Thus, and thus alone, it lays hold on eternal life; sometimes sacramentally, under external images and accidents; sometimes mystically, in the communion of deep prayer. "Every time we think with love of the Well-beloved, He is anew our meat and drink"—more, we too are His, for the love between God and man is a mutual love and desire. As we lay hold upon the Divine Life, devour and assimilate it, so in that very act the Divine Life devours us, and knits us up into the mystical Body of Reality. "Thou shalt not change Me into thine own substance, as thou dost change the food of thy flesh, but thou shalt be changed into Mine," said the Spirit of God to St. Augustine; and his Flemish descendant announces this same mysterious principle of life with greater richness and beauty.

"It is the nature of love ever to give and to take, to love and to be loved, and these two things meet in whomsoever loves. Thus the love of Christ is both avid and generous . . . as He devours us, so He would feed us.

[1] *The Mirror of Eternal Salvation*, cap. xvii.

If He absorbs us utterly into Himself, in return He gives us His very self again."[1]

This is but another aspect of that great 'inbreathing and outbreathing' of the Divine nature which governs the relation between the Creator and the flux of life; for Ruysbroeck's Christological language always carries with it the idea of the Logos, the Truth and Wisdom of Deity, as revealed in the world of conditions,—not only in the historical Jesus, but also in the eternal generation of the Son. St. Francis of Assisi had said that Divine Love perpetually swings between and reconciles two mighty opposites: "What is God? and, What am I?" For Ruysbroeck, too, that Love is a unifying power, manifested in motion itself, "an outgoing attraction, which drags us out of ourselves and calls us to be melted and naughted in the Unity";[2] and all his deepest thoughts of it are expressed in terms of movement.

The relation between the soul and the Absolute, then, is a love relation—as in fact all the mystics have declared it to be. Man, that imperfectly real thing, has an inherent tendency towards God, the Only Reality. Already possessed of a life within the world of conditions, his unquiet heart reaches out towards a world that transcends conditions. How shall he achieve that world?

[1] *Op. cit.*, cap. vii.
[2] *The Sparkling Stone*, cap. x.

In the same way, says Ruysbroeck, as the child achieves the world of manhood: by the double method of growth and education, the balanced action of the organism and its environment. In its development and its needs, spirit conforms to the great laws of natural life. Taught by the voices of the forest and that inward Presence who 'spoke without utterance' in his soul, he is quick to recognise the close parallels between nature and grace. His story of the mystical life is the story of birth, growth, adolescence, maturity: a steady progress, dependent on food and nurture, on the 'brooks of grace' which flow from the Living Fountain and bring perpetual renovation to help the wise disciplines and voluntary choices that brace and purge our expanding will and love.

Ruysbroeck's universe, like that of Kabir and certain other great mystics, has three orders: Becoming, Being, God. Parallel with this, he distinguishes three great stages in the soul's achievement of complete reality: the Active, the Interior, and the Superessential Life, sometimes symbolised by the conditions of Servant, Friend, and Son of God. These, however, must be regarded rather as divisions made for convenience of description, answering to those divisions which thought has made in the indivisible fact of the universe, than as

distinctions inherent in the reality of things.
The spiritual life has the true character of
duration; it is one indivisible tendency
and movement towards our source and
home, in which the past is never left behind,
but incorporated in the larger present.

In the Active Life, the primary interest
is ethical. Man here purifies his normal
human correspondences with the world of
sense, approximates his will to the Will of
God. Here, his contacts with the Divine
take place within that world of sense, and
'by means.' In the Interior Life, the
interest embraces the intellect, upon which
is now conferred the vision of Reality. As
the Active Life corresponded to the world of
Becoming, this Life corresponds with the
supersensual world of Being, where the
self's contacts with the Divine take place
'without means.' In the Superessential Life,
the self has transcended the intellectual
plane and entered into the very heart of
Reality; where she does not behold, but
has fruition of, God in one life and one love.
The obvious parallel between these three
stages and the traditional 'threefold way'
of Purgation, Illumination and Union is,
however, not so exact as it appears. Many
of the characters of the Unitive Way are
present in Ruysbroeck's 'second life'; and
his 'third life' takes the soul to heights
of fruition which few amongst even the

greatest unitive mystics have attained or described.

(A) When man first feels upon his soul the touch of the Divine Light, at once, and in a moment of time, his will is changed; turned in the direction of Reality and away from unreal objects of desire. He is, in fact, 'converted' in the highest and most accurate sense of that ill-used word. Seeing the Divine, he wants the Divine, though he may not yet understand his own craving; for the scrap of Divine Life within him has emerged into the field of consciousness, and recognises its home. Then, as it were, God and the soul rush together, and of their encounter springs love. This is the New Birth; the 'bringing forth of the Son in the ground of the soul,' its baptism in the fountain of the Life-giving Life.

The new force and tendency received into the self begins to act on the periphery, and thence works towards the centre of existence. First, then, it attacks the ordinary temporal life in all its departments. It pours in fresh waves of energy which confer new knowledge and hatred of sin, purify character, bring fresh virtues into being. It rearranges the consciousness about new and higher centres, gathering up all the faculties into one simple state of 'attention to God.' Thence results the highest life which is attainable by 'nature.' In it, man is united with God 'through means,' acts in obedience to the dictates of Divine Love and in accordance with the tendency of the Divine Will, and becomes the 'Faithful Servant' of the Transcendent Order. Plainly, the Active Life, thus considered, has much in common with the 'Purgative Way' of ascetic science.

(B) When this growth has reached its term, when "Free-will wears the crown of Charity, and rules as a King over the soul," the awakened and enhanced consciousness begins to crave a closer contact with the spiritual: that unmediated and direct contact which is the essence of the Contemplative or Interior Life, and is achieved in the deep state of recollection called 'unitive prayer.' Here voluntary and purposive education takes its place by the side of organic development. The way called by most ascetic writers 'Illumination'—the state of 'proficient' in monastic parlance—includes the *training* of the self in the contemplative art as well as its *growth* in will and love. This training braces and purifies intellect, as the disciplines of the active life purified will and sense. It teaches introversion, or the turning inward of the attention from the distractions of the sense-world; the cleansing of the mirror of thought, thronged with confusing images; the production of that silence in which the music of the Infinite can be heard. Nor is the Active Life here left behind; it is carried up to, and included in, the new, deepened activities of the self, which are no longer ruled by the laws, but by the 'quickening counsels' of God.

Of this new life, interior courage is a first necessity. It is no easy appropriation of supersensual graces, but a deeper entering into the mystery of life, a richer, more profound, participation in pain, effort, as well as joy. There must be no settling down into a comfortable sense of the Divine Presence, no reliance on the 'One Act'; but an incessant process of change, renewal, re-emergence. Sometimes Ruysbroeck appears to see this central stage in the spiritual life-process in terms of upward growth toward transcendent levels; sometimes in terms of recollection, the steadfast pressing inwards of consciousness towards that bare ground of the soul where it unites with immanent Reality, and finds the Divine Life surging up like a 'living fountain' from the deeps. This double way of conceiving one process is puzzling for us; but a proof that for Ruysbroeck no one concept could suggest the whole truth, and a useful reminder of the symbolic character of all these maps and itineraries of the spiritual life.

As the sun grows in power with the passing

seasons, so the soul now experiences a steady increase in the power and splendour of the Divine Light, as it ascends in the heavens of consciousness and pours its heat and radiance into all the faculties of man. The in-beating of this energy and light brings the self into the tempestuous heats of high summer, or full illumination—the 'fury of love,' most fertile and dangerous epoch of the spiritual year. Thence, obedient to those laws of movement, that 'double rhythm of renunciation and love' which Kabir detected at the heart of the universal melody, it enters on a negative period of psychic fatigue and spiritual destitution; the 'dark night of the soul.' The sun descends in the heavens, the ardours of love grow cold. When this stage is fully established, says Ruysbroeck, the 'September of the soul' is come; the harvest and vintage — raw material of the life-giving Eucharist — is ripe. The flowering-time of spiritual joy and beauty is as nothing in its value for life compared with this still autumnal period of true fecundity, in which man is at last 'affirmed' in the spiritual life.

This, then, is the curve of the self's growth. Side by side with it runs the other curve of deliberate training: the education by which our wandering attention, our diffused undisciplined consciousness, is sharpened and focussed upon Reality. This training is needed

by intellect and feeling; but most of all by
the *will*, which Ruysbroeck, like the great
English mystics, regards as the gathering-
point of personality, the 'spiritual heart.'
On every page of his writings the reference
to that which the spiritual Light and Love
do for man, is balanced by an insistence on
that which man himself must do: the choices
to be made, the 'exercises' to be performed,
the tension and effort which must characterise the mystic way until its last phase
is reached. Morally, these exercises consist
in progressive renunciations on the one hand
and acceptances on the other 'for Love's
sake'; intellectually, in introversion, that
turning inwards and concentration of consciousness, the stripping off of all images
and emptying of the mind, which is the psychological method whereby human consciousness transcends the conditioned universe
to which it has become adapted, and enters
the contemplative world. Man's attention to
life is to change its character as he ascends
the ladder of being. Therefore the old attachments must be cut before the new attachments
can be formed. This is, of course, a common-
place of asceticism; and much of Ruysbroeck's teaching on detachment, self-naughting and contemplation, is indeed simply the
standard doctrine of Christian asceticism seen
through a temperament.

When the self has grown up from the

'active' to the 'contemplative' state of consciousness, it is plain that his whole relation to his environment has changed. His world is grouped about a new centre. It now becomes the supreme business of intellect to 'gaze upon God,' the supreme business of love to stretch out towards Him. When these twin powers, under the regnancy of the enhanced and trained will, are set towards Reality, then the human creature has done his part in the setting up of the relation of the soul to its Source, and made it possible for the music of the Infinite to sound in him. "For this intellectual gazing and this stretching forth of love are two heavenly pipes, sounding without the need of tune or of notes; they ever go forward in that Eternal Life, neither straying aside nor returning backward again; and ever keeping harmony and concord with the Holy Church, for the Holy Spirit gives the wind that sings in them."[1] Observe, that *tension* is here a condition of the right employment of both faculties, and ensures that the Divine music shall sound true; one of the many implicit contradictions of the quietist doctrine of spiritual limpness, which we find throughout Ruysbroeck's works.

(C) When the twofold process of growth and education has brought the self to this perfection of attitude as regards the Spiritual Order—an attitude of true *union*, says Ruys-

[1] *The Twelve Béguines*, cap. xiv.

broeck, but not yet of the unthinkable *unity*
which is our goal—man has done all that he
can do of himself. His ' Interior Life ' is complete, and his being is united through grace
with the Being of God, in a relation which
is the faint image of the mutual relations of
the Divine Persons; a conscious sonship,
finding expression in the mutual interchange
of the spirit of will and love. This existence
is rooted in ' grace,' the unconditioned life-
force, ' intermediary between ourselves and
God,' as the active stage was rooted in
' nature.' Yet there is something beyond
this. As beyond the Divine Persons there
is the Superessential Unity of the Godhead,
so beyond the plane of Being (*Wesen*) Ruysbroeck apprehends a reality which is 'more
than Being ' (*Overwesen*). Man's spirit, having
relations with every grade of reality, has
also in its ' fathomless ground ' a potential
relation with this superessential sphere ; and
until this be actualised he is not wholly
real, nor wholly *deiform*. Ruysbroeck's
most original contribution to the history of
mysticism is his description of this supreme
state; in which the human soul becomes
truly free, and is made the ' hidden child '
of God. Then only do we discern the glory
of our full-grown human nature ; when,
participating fully in the mysterious double
life of God, the twofold action of true love,
we have perfect fruition of Him as Eternal

Rest, and perfect sharing in that outgoing love which is His eternal Work: " God with God, one love and one life, in His eternal manifestation." [1]

The consummation of the mystic way, then, represents not merely a state of ecstatic contemplation, escape from the stream of succession, the death of self-hood, joyous self-immersion in the Abyss; not merely the enormously enhanced state of creative activity and energetic love which the mystics call ' divine fecundity '; but *both*—the flux and reflux of supreme Reality. It is the synthesis of contemplation and action, of Being and Becoming: the discovery at last of a clue—inexpressible indeed, but really held and experienced—to the mystery which most deeply torments us, the link between our life of duration and the Eternal Life of God. This is the Seventh Degree of Love, " noblest and highest that can be realised in the life of time or of eternity."

That process of enhancement whereby the self, in its upward progress, carries with it all that has been attained before, here finds its completion. The active life of Becoming, and the essential life of Being, are not all. " From beyond the Infinite the Infinite comes," said the Indian; and his Christian brother, in parallel terms, declares that beyond the Essence is the Superessence of

[1] *The Twelve Béguines*, cap. xiii.

HIS DOCTRINE OF MAN

God, His 'simple' or synthetic unity. It is for fruition of this that man is destined; yet he does not leave this world for that world, but knows them as one. Totally surrendered to the double current of the universe, the inbreathing and outbreathing of the Spirit of God, "his love and fruition live between labour and rest." He goes up and down the mountain of vision, a living willing tool wherewith God works. "Hence, to enter into restful fruition and come forth again in good works, and to remain ever one with God—this is the thing that I would say. Even as we open our fleshly eyes to see, and shut them again so quickly that we do not even feel it, thus we die into God, we live of God, and remain ever one with God. Therefore we must come forth in the activities of the sense-life, and again re-enter in love and cling to God; in order that we may ever remain one with Him without change."[1]

All perfect lives, says Ruysbroeck, conform to this pattern, follow this curve; though such perfect lives are rare amongst men. They are the fruit, not of volition, but of vocation; of the mysterious operations of the Divine Light which—perpetually crying through the universe the "unique and fathomless word 'Behold! behold!'" and "therewith giving utterance to itself and all other things"—yet evokes only in some men an

[1] *The Seven Degrees of Love*, cap. xiv.

answering movement of consciousness, the deliberate surrender which conditions the new power of response and of growth. "To this divine vision but few men can attain, because of their own unfitness and because of the darkness of that Light whereby we see: and therefore no one shall thoroughly understand this perception by means of any scholarship, or by their own acuteness of comprehension. For all words, and all that men may learn and understand in a creaturely fashion, is foreign to this and far below the truth that I mean. To understand and lay hold of God as He is in Himself above all images—this is *to be God with God*, without intermediary or any difference that might become an intermediary or an obstacle. And therefore I beg each one, who can neither understand this, nor feel it by the way of spiritual union, that he be not grieved thereby, and let it be as it is."[1]

I end this chapter by a reference to certain key-words frequent in Ruysbroeck's works, which are sometimes a source of difficulty to his readers. These words are nearly always his names for inward experiences. He uses them in a poetic and artistic manner, evocative rather than exact; and we, in trying to discover their meaning, must never forget the coloured fringe of suggestion which they carry for the mystic and the

[1] *The Spiritual Marriage*, lib. iii. cap. i.

poet, and which is a true part of the message he intends them to convey.

The first of these words is FRUITION. Fruition, a concept which Eucken's philosophy has brought back into current thought, represents a total attainment, complete and permanent participation and possession. It is an absolute state, transcending all succession, and it is applied by Ruysbroeck to the absolute character of the spirit's life in God; which, though it seem to the surface consciousness a perpetually renewed encounter of love, is in its ground 'fruitive and unconditioned,' a timeless self-immersion in the Dark, the 'glorious and essential Oneness.' Thus he speaks of 'fruitive love,' 'fruitive possession'; as opposed to striving, dynamic love, partial, progressive and conditioned possession. Perfect contemplation and loving dependence are the 'eternal fruition of God': the Beatific Vision of theology. "Where we are one with God, without intermediary, beyond all separation; there is God our fruition and His own in an eternal and fathomless bliss." [1]

Next perhaps in the power of provoking misunderstanding is the weight attached by Ruysbroeck to the adjective SIMPLE. This word, which constantly recurs in his descriptions of spiritual states, always conveys the sense of wholeness, completeness, syn-

[1] *The Twelve Béguines*, cap. xvi.

thesis; not of poverty, thinness, subtraction. It is the white light in which all the colours of the spectrum are included and fused. 'Simple Union,' 'Simple Contemplation,' 'Simple Light'—all these mean the total undifferentiated act or perception from which our analytic minds subtract aspects. "In simplicity will I unite with the Simple One," said Kabir. So Ruysbroeck: "We behold His face in a simple seeing, beyond reason and without consideration."

Another cause of difficulty to those unfamiliar with the mystics is the constant reference to BARENESS or NUDITY, especially in descriptions of the contemplative act. This is, of course, but one example of that negative method of suggestion—darkness, bareness, desolation, divine ignorance, the 'rich nothing,' the 'naked thought '—which is a stock device of mysticism, and was probably taken by Ruysbroeck from Dionysius the Areopagite. It represents, first, the bewildering emptiness and nakedness of consciousness when introduced into a universe that transcends our ordinary conceptual world; secondly, the necessity of such transcendence, of emptying the field of consciousness of 'every vain imagining,' if the self is to have contact with the Reality which these veil.

With the distinction between Essence (*Wesen*) and Superessence (*Overwesen*) I have

HIS DOCTRINE OF MAN

already dealt; and this will appear more clearly when we consider Ruysbroeck's 'second' and 'third' stages of the mystic life.

There remains the great pair of opposites, fundamental for his thought, called in the Flemish vernacular *Wise* and *Onwise*, and generally rendered by translators as 'Mode' and 'Modeless.' Wherever possible I have replaced these tasteless Latinisms by the Old English equivalents 'in some wise' and 'in no wise,' occasionally by 'conditioned' and 'unconditioned'; though perhaps the colloquial 'somehow' and 'nohow' would be yet more exactly expressive. Now this pair of opposites is psychological rather than metaphysical, and has to do with the characteristic phenomena of contemplation. It indicates the difference between the universe of the normal man, living as the servant or friend of God within the temporal order, and the universe of the true contemplative, the 'hidden child.' The knowledge and love of the first is a conditioned knowledge and love. Everything which happens to him happens 'in some wise'; it has attachments within his conceptual world, is mediated to him by symbols and images which intellect can grasp. "The simple ascent into the Nude and the Unconditioned is unknown and unloved of him"; it is through and amongst his ordinary mental furniture that he obtains his contacts with Reality. But the knowledge and love of the second, his contacts, transcend the categories of thought. He has escaped alike from the tyrannies and comforts of the world of images, has made the 'ascent into the Nought,' where all *is*, yet 'in no wise.' "The power of the understanding is lifted up to that which is beyond all conditions, and its seeing is in no wise, being without manner, and it is neither thus nor thus, neither here nor there." [1] This is the direct, unmediated world of spiritual intuition; where the self touches a Reality that has not been passed through the filters of sense and thought. There man achieves a love, a vision, an activity which are 'wayless,' yet far more valid than anything that can be fitted into the framework of our conditioned world.

"In a place beyond uttermost place, in a track without shadow of trace,
Soul and body transcending, I live in the soul of my Loved One anew."

Thus cries the great Sūfī poet, Jalālu'ddīn; and the suggestion which his words convey is perhaps as close as speech can come to what Ruysbroeck meant by *Onwise*. The change of consciousness which initiates man into this inner yet unbounded world—the world that is 'unwalled,' to use his own

[1] *The Twelve Bêguines*, cap. xii.

HIS DOCTRINE OF MAN

favourite metaphor—is the essence of contemplation; which consists, not in looking at strange mysteries, but in a movement to fresh levels, shut to the analytic intellect, open to adventurous love. There, without any amazement, the self can 'know in no wise' that which it can never understand.

> "Contemplation is a knowing that is in no wise,
> For ever dwelling above the Reason.
> Never can it sink down into the Reason,
> And above it can the Reason never climb.
> The shining forth of That which is in no wise is as a fair mirror,
> Wherein shines the Eternal Light of God.
> It has no attributes,
> And here all the works of Reason fail.
> It is not God,
> But it is the Light whereby we see Him.
> Those who walk in the Divine Light of it
> Discover in themselves the Unwalled.
> That which is in no wise, is above the Reason, not without it:
> It beholds all things without amazement.
> Amazement is far beneath it:
> The contemplative life is without amazement.
> That which is in no wise sees, it knows not what;
> For it is above all, and is neither This nor That."[1]

---

[1] *The Twelve Béguines*, cap. viii.

CHAPTER V

THE ACTIVE LIFE

If we would discover and know that Kingdom of God which is hidden in us, we must lead a life that is virtuous within, well-ordered without, and fulfilled with true charity. Thus imitating Christ in every way, we can, through grace, love and virtue, raise ourselves up to that apex of the soul where God lives and reigns.
THE MIRROR OF ETERNAL SALVATION.

THE beginning of man's Active Life, says Ruysbroeck—that uplifting of the diurnal existence into the Divine Atmosphere, which confers on it meaning and reality — is a movement of response. Grace, the synthesis of God's love, energy and will, pours like a great river through the universe, and perpetually beats in upon the soul. When man consents to receive it, opens the sluices of the heart to that living water, surrenders to it; then he opens his heart and will to the impact of Reality, his eyes to the Divine Light, and in this energetic movement of acceptance begins for the first time to live indeed. Hence it is that, in the varied ethical systems which we find in his books, and which describe the active crescent life of Christian virtue, the laborious adjustment of character to the Vision of God, Ruysbroeck always puts first the virtue, or rather the attitude, which he calls *good-will:* the voluntary orientation of the self in the right direction, the eager acceptance of grace. As all growth depends upon food, so all spiritual development depends upon the self's appropriation of its own share of the transcendent life-force, its own ' rill of grace '; and good-will breaks down the barrier which prevents that stream from pouring into the soul.

Desire, said William Law, *is* everything and *does* everything; it is the primal motive-power. Ruysbroeck, too, finds in desire turned towards the best the beginning of human transcendence, and regards willing and loving as the essence of life. Basing his psychology on the common mediæval scheme of Memory, Intelligence and Will, he speaks of this last as the king of the soul; dominating both the other powers, and able to gather them in its clutch, force them to attend to the invitations and messages of the eternal world. Thus in his system the demand upon man's industry and courage is made from the very first. The great mystical necessity of self-surrender is shown to involve, not a limp acquiescence, but a deliberate and heroic choice; the difficult approximation of our own thoughts and desires to the thoughts and desires of Divine Reality. "When we have but one thought and one will with God, we are on the first step of the ladder of love and of sanctity; for good-will is the foundation of all virtue." [1]

In *The Adornment of the Spiritual Marriage*, Ruysbroeck has used the words said to the wise and foolish virgins of the parable— "Behold, the bridegroom cometh; go ye out to meet him"—as an epitome of the self's relations with and reactions to Reality. First, all created spirits are called to behold God, who is perpetually 'coming' to the world of conditions, in a ceaseless procession of love; and in this seeing our happiness consists. But in order really to see a thing, we need not only light and clear sight, but the *will* to look at it; every act of perception demands a self-giving on the seer's part. So here we need not only the light of grace and the open eyes of the soul, but also the *will* turned towards the Infinite: our attention to life, the regnant fact of our consciousness, must be focussed upon eternal things. Now, when we see God, we cannot but love Him; and love is motion, activity. Hence, this first demand on the awakened spirit, 'Behold!' is swiftly followed by the second demand, 'Go ye out!' for the essence of love is generous, outflowing, expansive,

[1] *The Seven Degrees of Love*, cap. i.

THE ACTIVE LIFE

an "upward and outward tendency towards the Kingdom of God, which is God Himself." This outgoing, this concrete act of response, will at once change and condition our correspondences with and attitude towards God, ourselves and our neighbours; expressing itself within the world of action in a new ardour for perfection—the natural result of the 'loving vision of the Bridegroom,' the self's first glimpse of Perfect Goodness and Truth. We observe the continued insistence on effort, act, as the very heart of all true self-giving to transcendent interests.

Whilst in the volitional life drastic readjustments, stern character-building, and eager work are the expression of goodwill, in the emotional life it is felt as a profound impulse to self-surrender: a loving yielding up of the whole personality to the inflow and purging activities of the Absolute Life. "This good-will is nought else but the infused Love of God, which causes him to apply himself to Divine things and all virtues; . . . when it turns towards God, it crowns the spirit with Eternal Love, and when it returns to outward things it rules as a mistress over his external good deeds." [1]

We have here, then, a disposition of heart and mind which both receives and responds

[1] *The Mirror of Eternal Salvation*, cap. xvi.

to the messages of Reality ; making it possible for the self to begin to grow in the right direction, to enter into possession of its twofold heritage. That completely human life of activity and contemplation which moves freely up and down the ladder of love between the temporal and eternal worlds, and reproduces in little the ideal of Divine Humanity declared in Christ, is the ideal towards which it is set ; and already, even in this lowest phase, the double movement of the awakened consciousness begins to show itself. Our love and will, firmly fastened in the Eternal World, are to swing like a pendulum between the seen and the unseen spheres ; in great ascending arcs of balanced adoration and service, which shall bring all the noblest elements of human character into play. Therefore the pivoting of life upon Divine Reality, which is the result of good-will—the setting up of a right relation with the universe—is inevitably the first condition of virtue, the ' root of sanctity,' the beginning of spiritual growth, the act which makes man free ; translating him, in Ruysbroeck's image, from the state of the slave to that of the conscious and willing servant of Eternal Truth. " From the hour in which, with God's help, he transcends his self-hood . . . he feels true love, which overcomes doubt and fear and makes man trust and hope; and so he becomes a true servant, and means and loves God in all that he does." [1]

So man, emerging from the shell of selfhood, makes—of his own free choice, by his own effort—his first timid upward beat to God; and, following swiftly upon it, the compensating outward beat of charity towards his fellow-men. We observe how tight a hold has this most transcendental of the mystics on the *wholeness* of all healthy human life : the mutual support and interpenetration of the active and contemplative powers. 'Other-worldliness' is decisively contradicted from the first. It is the appearance of this eager active charity —this imitation in little of the energetic Love of God—which assures us that the first stage of the self's growth is rightly accomplished; completing its first outward push in that new direction to which its good-will is turned. "For charity ever presses towards the heights, towards the Kingdom of God, the which is God Himself."

In the practical counsels given to the young novice to whom *The Mirror of Salvation* is addressed, we may see Ruysbroeck's ideal of that active life of self-discipline and service which the soul has now set in hand; and which he describes in greater

[1] *The Sparkling Stone*, cap. vi.

detail in *The Adornment of the Spiritual Marriage* and *The Kingdom of God's Lovers*. Total self-donation, he tells her, is her first need—'choosing God, for love's sake' without hesitations or reserves; and this dedication to the interests of Reality must be untainted by any spiritual selfishness, any hint of that insidious desire for personal beatitude which 'fades the flower of true love.' This done, self-conquest and self-control become the novice's primary duties: the gradual subduing and re-arrangement of character about its new centre, the elimination of all tendencies inimical to the demands of Eternal Life; the firm establishment upon its throne of that true free-will which desires only God's will. This self-conquest, the essence of the 'Way of Purgation,' as described and experienced by so many ascetics and mystics, includes not only the eradication of sins, but the training of the attention, the adaptation of consciousness to its new environment; the killing-out of inclinations which, harmless in themselves, compete with the one transcendent interest of life.

Like all great mystics, Ruysbroeck had a strong 'sense of sin.' This is merely a theological way of stating the fact that his intense realisation of Perfection involved a vivid consciousness of the imperfections, disharmonies, perversities, implicit in the human creature; the need of resolving them if the soul was to grow up to the stature of Divine Humanity. Yet there is in his writings a singular absence of that profound preoccupation with sin found in so many mediæval ascetics. His attitude towards character was affirmative and robust; emphasising the possibilities rather than the disabilities of man. Sin, for him, was egotism; showing itself in the manifold forms of pride, laziness, self-indulgence, coldness of heart, or spiritual self-seeking, but always implying a central wrongness of attitude, resulting in a wrong employment of power. Self-denials and bodily mortifications he regarded partly as exercises in self-control—spiritual athletics—useful because educative of the will; partly as expressions of love. At best they are but the means of sanctity, and never to be confused with its end; for the man who deliberately passed the greater part of his life in the bustle of the town was no advocate of a cloistered virtue or a narrow perfectionism.

Morbid piety is often the product of physical as well as spiritual stuffiness; and Ruysbroeck wrote his great books out of doors, with light and air all round him, and the rhythmic life of trees to remind him how much stronger was the quiet law of growth than any atavism, accident, or perversion by which it could be checked. Thus, throughout his works, the accent always falls upon power rather than weakness : upon the spiritual energy pouring in like sunshine ; the incessant growth which love sets going ; the perpetual rebirths to ever higher levels, as the young sapling stretches upward every spring. What he asks of the novice is contrition without anxiety, self-discipline without fuss ; the steady, all-round development of her personality, stretching and growing towards God. She is to be the mistress of her soul, never permitting it to be drawn hither and thither by the distractions and duties of external life. Keeping always in the atmosphere of Reality, she shall bring therefrom truth and frankness to all her words and deeds ; and perform her duties with that right and healthy detachment which springs, not from a contempt of the Many, but from the secure and loving possession of the One.

The disciplines to which she must subject herself in the effort towards attainment of this poise, will, like a wise gymnastic, produce in her a suppleness of soul ; making the constant and inevitable transition from interior communion to outward work, which charity and good sense demand, easy and natural, and causing the spirit to be plastic in the hand of God. Such suppleness—the lightness and lissomeness which comes from

spiritual muscles exercised and controlled—
was one of the favourite qualities of that
wise trainer of character, St. François de
Sales; and the many small and irritating
mortifications with which he was accustomed to torment his disciples had no
other aim than to produce it.

In the stage of development to which the
Active Life belongs, the soul enjoys communion with Reality, not with that directness proper to the true contemplative, but
obliquely, by 'means,' symbols and images;
especially by the sacramental dispensation
of the Church, a subject to which Ruysbroeck devotes great attention. As always
in his system, growth from within is intimately connected with the reception of food
and power from without. The movement
of the self into God, the movement of God
into the self, though separable in thought,
are one in fact: will and grace are two
aspects of one truth. Only this paradox
can express the relation between that Divine
Love which is 'both avid and generous,'
and the self that is destined both to devour
and be devoured by Reality

In the beautiful chapters on the Eucharist
which form the special feature of *The
Mirror of Eternal Salvation*, Ruysbroeck
develops this idea. "If He gives us all
that He has and all that He is, in return He
takes from us all that we have and all that

we are, and demands of us more than we are capable of giving. . . . Even in devouring us, He desires to feed us. If He absorbs us utterly into Himself, He gives Himself in return. He causes to be born in us the hunger and thirst of the spirit, which shall make us savour Him in an eternal fruition; and to this spiritual hunger, as well as to the love of our heart, He gives His own Body as food. . . . Thus does He give us His life full of wisdom, truth and knowledge, in order that we may imitate Him in all virtues; and then He lives in us and we in Him. Then do we grow, and raise ourselves up above the reason into a Divine Love which causes us to take and consume that Food in a spiritual manner, and stretch out in pure love towards the Divinity. There takes place that encounter of the spirit, that is to say of measureless love, which consumes and transforms our spirit with all its works; drawing us with itself towards the Unity, where we taste beatitude and rest. Herein therefore is our eternal life : ever to devour and be devoured, to ascend and descend with love." [1]

The soul, then, turned in the direction of the Infinite, ' having God for aim,' and with her door opened to the inflowing Divine Life, begins to grow. Her growth is up and out; from that temporal world to which

[1] *The Mirror of Eternal Salvation*, cap. vii.

her nature is adapted, and where she seems full of power and efficiency, to that eternal world to which the 'spark' within her belongs, but where she is as yet no more than a weak and helpless child. Hence the first state of mind and heart produced in her, if the ' new birth ' has indeed taken place, will be that humility which results from all real self-knowledge; since " whoso might verily see and feel himself as he *is*, he should verily be meek." This clear acknowledgment of facts, this finding of one's own place, Ruysbroeck calls ' the solid foundation of the Kingdom of the Soul.' In thus discerning love and humility as the governing characteristics of the soul's reaction to Reality, he is of course keeping close to the great tradition of Christian mysticism; especially to the teaching of Richard of St. Victor, which we find constantly repeated in the ascetic literature of the Middle Ages.

From these two virtues, then, of humble self-knowledge and God-centred love, are gradually developed all those graces of character which ' adorn the soul for the spiritual marriage,' mark her ascent of the first degrees of the ' ladder of love,' and make possible the perfecting of her correspondences with the ' Kingdom.' This development follows an orderly course, as subject to law as the unfolding of the leaves and flowers upon the growing plant; and though Ruysbroeck in his various works uses different diagrams wherewith to explain it, the psychological changes which these diagrams demonstrate are substantially the same. In each case we watch the opening of man's many-petalled heart under the rays of the Divine Light, till it blossoms at last into the rose of Perfect Charity.

Thus in *The Seven Degrees of Love*, since he is there addressing a cloistered nun, he accommodates his system to that threefold monastic vow of voluntary poverty or perfect renunciation, chastity or singleness of heart, and obedience or true humility in action, by which she is bound. When the reality which these vows express is actualised in the soul, and dominates all her reactions to the world, she wears the ' crown of virtue ' ; and lives that ' noble life ' ruled by the purified and enhanced will, purged of all selfish desires and distractions, which —seeking in all things the interests of the spiritual world—is ' full of love and charity, and industrious in good works.'

In *The Spiritual Marriage* a more elaborate analysis is possible ; based upon that division of man's moral perversities into the ' seven mortal sins ' or seven fundamental forms of selfishness, which governed, and governs yet, the Catholic view of human character. After a preliminary passage in which the triple attitude of love as towards

God, humility as towards self, justice as towards other men, is extolled as the only secure basis of the spiritual life, Ruysbroeck proceeds to exhibit the seven real and positive qualities which oppose the seven great abuses of human freedom. As Pride is first and worst of mortal sins and follies, so its antithesis Humility is again put forward as the first condition of communion with God. This produces in the emotional life an attitude of loving adoration; in the volitional life, obedience. By *obedience*, Ruysbroeck means that self-submission, that wise suppleness of spirit, which is swayed and guided not by its own tastes and interests but by the Will of God; as expressed in the commands and prohibitions of moral and spiritual law, the interior push of conscience. This attitude, at first deliberately assumed, gradually controls all the self's reactions, and ends by subduing it entirely to the Divine purpose. "Of this obedience there grows the abdication of one's own will and one's own opinion; ... by this abdication of the will in all that one does, or does not do, or endures, the substance and occasion of pride are wholly driven out, and the highest humility is perfected."[1]

This movement of renunciation brings—next phase in the unselfing of the self—a com-

[1] *The Spiritual Marriage*, lib. i. cap. xiv.

pensating outward swing of love; expressed under the beautiful forms of *patience*, 'the tranquil tolerance of all that can happen,' and hence the antithesis of Anger; *gentleness*, which "with peace and calm bears vexatious words and deeds"; *kindness*, which deals with the quarrelsome and irritable by means of "a friendly countenance, affectionate persuasion and compassionate acts"; and *sympathy*, "that inward movement of the heart which compassionates the bodily and spiritual griefs of all men," and kills the evil spirit of Envy and hate. This fourfold increase in disinterested love is summed up in the condition which Ruysbroeck calls *supernatural generosity;* that largeness of heart which flows out towards the generosity of God, which is swayed by pity and love, which embraces all men in its sweep. By this energetic love which seeks not its own, "all virtues are increased, and all the powers of the spirit are adorned"; and Avarice, the fourth great mortal sin, is opposed.

Generosity is no mere mood; it is a motive-force, demanding expression in action. From the emotions, it invades the will, and produces *diligence* and *zeal:* an 'inward and impatient eagerness' for every kind of work, and for the hard practice of every kind of virtue, which makes impossible that slackness and dulness of

THE ACTIVE LIFE

soul which is characteristic of the sin of Sloth. It is dynamic love; and the spirit which is fired by its ardours, has reached a degree of self-conquest in which the two remaining evil tendencies—that to every kind of immoderate enjoyment, spiritual, intellectual or physical, which is the essence of Gluttony, and that to the impure desire of created things which is Lust—can be met and vanquished. The purged and strengthened will, crowned by unselfish love, is now established on its throne; man has become captain of his soul, and rules all the elements of his character and that character's expression in life — not as an absolute monarch, but in the name of Divine Love.[1] He has done all he can do of himself towards the conforming of his life to Supreme Perfection; has opposed, one after another, each of those exhibitions of the self's tendency to curl inwards, to fence itself in and demand, absorb, enjoy as a separate entity, which lie at the root of sin. The constructive side of the Purgative Way has consisted in the replacement of this egoistic, indrawing energy by these outflowing energies of self-surrender, kindness, diligence and the rest; summed up in that perfection of humility and love, which "in all its works, and always, stretches out towards God."

[1] *The Spiritual Marriage*, lib. i. capp. xii.–xxiv.

The first three gifts of the Holy Spirit are possessed by the soul which has reached this point, says Ruysbroeck in *The Kingdom of God's Lovers:* that loving Fear, which includes true humility with all its ancillary characteristics; that general attitude of charity which makes man gentle, patient and docile, ready to serve and pity every one, and is called Godliness, because there first emerges in it his potential likeness to God; and finally that Knowledge or discernment of right and prudent conduct which checks the disastrous tendency to moral fussiness, helps man to conform his life to supreme Perfection, and gives the calmness and balance which are essential to a sane and manly spirituality. Thus the new life-force has invaded and affected will, feeling and intellect; raised the whole man to fresh levels of existence, and made possible fresh correspondences with Reality. "Hereby are the three lower powers of the soul adorned with Divine virtues. The Irascible [*i.e.* volitional and dynamic] is adorned with loving and filial fear, humility, obedience and renunciation. The Desirous is adorned with kindness, pity, compassion and generosity. Finally, the Reasonable with knowledge and discernment, and that prudence which regulates all things."[1] The ideal of character held out and described under

[1] *The Kingdom of God's Lovers,* cap. xviii.

varying metaphors in Ruysbroeck's different works, is thus seen to be a perfectly consistent one.

Now when the growing self has actualised this ideal, and lives the Active Life of the faithful servant of Reality, it begins to feel an ardent desire for some more direct encounter with That which it loves. Since it has now acquired the 'ornaments of the virtues'—cleansed its mirror, ordered its disordered loves—this encounter may and does in a certain sense take place; for every Godward movement of the human is met by a compensating movement of the Divine. Man now begins to find God in all things: in nature, in the soul, in works of charity. But in the turmoil and bustle of the Active Life such an encounter is at best indirect; a sidelong glimpse of the 'first and only Fair.' That vision can only be apprehended in its wholeness by a concentration of all the powers of the self. If we would look the Absolute in the eyes, we must look at nothing else; the complete opening of the eye of Eternity entails the closing of the eye of Time. Man, then, must abstract himself from multiplicity, if only for a moment, if he would catch sight of the Unspeakable Simplicity of the Real. Longing to 'know the nature of the Beloved,' he must act as Zacchæus did when he wished to see Christ :

"He must run before the crowd, that is to say the multiplicity of created things; for these make us so little and low that we cannot perceive God. And he must climb up on the Tree of Faith, which grows from above downwards, for its root is in the Godhead. This tree has twelve branches, which are the twelve articles of the Creed. The lower branches speak of the Humanity of God; . . . the upper branches, however, speak of the Godhead: of the Trinity of Persons and the Unity of the Divine Nature. Man must cling to the Unity which is at the top of the tree, for it is here that Jesus will pass by with all His gifts. And now Jesus comes, and He sees man, and shows him in the light of faith that He is, according to His Divinity, unmeasured and incomprehensible, inaccessible and fathomless, and that He overpasses all created light and all finite comprehension. This is the highest knowledge of God which man can acquire in the Active Life: thus to recognise by the light of faith that God is inconceivable and unknowable. In this light God says to the desire of man: "Come down quickly, for I would dwell in your house to-day." And this quick descent, to which God invites him, is nought else but a descent, by love and desire, into the Abyss of the Godhead, to which no intellect can attain by its created light. But here, where intellect must rest without, love and desire may enter in. When the soul thus leans upon God by intention and love, above all that she understands, then she rests and dwells in God, and God in her. When the soul mounts up by desire, above the multiplicity of things, above the activities of the senses and above the light of external nature, then she encounters Christ by the light of faith, and is illuminated; and she recognises that God is unknowable and inconceivable. Finally, stretching by desire towards this incomprehensible God, she meets Christ and is fulfilled with His gifts. And loving and resting above all gifts, above herself and above all things, she dwells in God and God in her. According to this manner Christ may be encountered upon the summit of the Active Life."[1]

This, then, is the completion of the first stage in the mystic way; this showing to the purified consciousness of the helplessness of the analytic intellect, the dynamic power of self-surrendered love. "Where intellect must rest without, love and desire may enter in." The human creature, turning towards Reality, has pressed up to the very edge of the 'Cloud of Unknowing' in which the goal of transcendence is hid. If it is to go further it must bring to the adventure not knowledge but divine ignorance, not riches

[1] *The Spiritual Marriage*, lib. i. cap. xxvi.

but poverty; above all, an eager and industrious love.

"A fiery flame of devotion leaping and ascending into the very goodness of God Himself,
A loving longing of the soul to be with God in His Eternity,
A turning from all things of self into the freedom of the Will of God;
With all the forces of the soul gathered into the unity of the spirit." [1]

---

[1] *The Twelve Béguines*, cap. vii.

CHAPTER VI

THE INTERIOR LIFE: ILLUMINATION AND DESTITUTION

Let whoso thirsts to see his God cleanse his mirror, purge his spirit; and when thus he has cleansed his mirror, and long and diligently gazed in it, a certain brightness of divine light begins to shine through upon him, and a certain immense ray of unwonted vision to appear before his eyes. . . . From the beholding of this light, which it sees within itself with amazement, the mind is mightily set on fire, and lifted up to behold that Light which is above itself.

RICHARD OF ST. VICTOR.

IT is plain that the Active Life in Ruysbroeck's system answers more or less to the Purgative Way, considered upon its affirmative and constructive side, as a building up of the heroic Christian character. So, too, the life which he calls Interior or Contemplative, and which initiates man into the friendship of God, corresponds in the main with the Illuminative Way of orthodox mysticism; though it includes in its later stages much that is usually held to belong to the third, or Unitive, state of the soul. The first life has, as it were, unfolded to the sunlight the outer petals of the mystic rose; exhibiting in their full beauty, adjusting to their true use, the normally-apparent constituents of man's personality. All his relations with the given world of sense, the sphere of Becoming, have been purified and adjusted. Now the expansive and educative influence of the Divine Light is able to penetrate nearer to the heart of his personality; is brought to bear upon those interior qualities which he hardly knows himself to possess, and which govern his relation with the spiritual world of Being. The flower is to open more widely; the inner ring of petals must uncurl.

As the primary interest of the Active Life was ethical purification, so the primary interest of this Second Life is intellectual purification. Intellect, however, is here to be understood in its highest sense; as including not only the analytic reason which deals with the problems of our normal universe, but that higher intelligence, that contemplative mind, which — once it is awakened to consciousness — can gather news of the transcendental world. The development and clarification of this power is only possible to those who have achieved, and continue to live at full stretch, the high, arduous and unselfish life of Christian virtue. Again we must remind ourselves that Ruysbroeck's theory of transcendence involves, not the passage from one life to another, but the *adding* of one life to another: the perpetual deepening, widening, heightening and enriching of human experience. As the author of *The Cloud of Unknowing* insists that none can be truly contemplative who is not also active, so Ruysbroeck says that no man ever rises above the ordinary obligations of Christian kindness and active good works.

"We find nowadays many silly men who would be so interior and so detached, that they will not be active or helpful in any way of which their neighbours are in need. Know, such men are neither hidden friends nor yet true servants of God, but are wholly false and disloyal; for none can follow His counsels but those who obey His laws."[1]

Nevertheless it would be generally true to say that, whilst the aim of the Active Life is right conduct, the aim of the Interior Life is right vision and thought. As, in that first life, all the perversions of man's ordinary powers and passions were rectified, all that was superfluous and unreal done away, and his nature set right with God; now—still holding and living in its fulness this purified active life—he is to press deeper and deeper into the resources of

[1] *The Sparkling Stone*, cap. vii.

his being, finding there other powers and cravings which must be brought within the field of consciousness, and set up those relations with the Transcendent of which they are capable. This deepening and enlarging of man's universe, together with the further and more drastic discarding of illusions and unrealities, is the business of the Second Life, considered on its impersonal side.

"If thou dost desire to unfold in thyself the Contemplative Life, thou must enter within, beyond the sense-life; and, on that apex of thy being, adorned with all the virtues of which I have spoken, looking unto God with gratitude and love and continual reverence, thou must keep thy thoughts bare, and stripped of every sensible image, thine understanding open and lifted up to the Eternal Truth, and thy spirit spread out in the sight of God as a living mirror to receive His everlasting likeness. Behold, therein appears a light of the understanding, which neither sense, reason, nature, nor the clearest logic can apprehend, but which gives us freedom and confidence towards God. It is nobler and higher than all that God has created in nature; for it is the perfection of nature, and transcends nature, and is the clear-shining intermediary between ourselves and God. Our thoughts, bare and stripped of images, are themselves the living mirror in which this light shines: and the light requires of us that we should be like to and one with God, in this living mirror of our bare thoughts."[1]

In this strongly Victorine passage, the whole process of the Second Life is epitomised; but in *The Spiritual Marriage*, where its description occupies the seventy-three chapters of the second book, we see how long is the way which stretches from that first 'entering in beyond the sense life' to the point at which the soul's mirror is able to receive in its fullness that Light wherein alone it can apprehend Reality.

Considered upon its organic side, as a growth and movement of the soul, this Way, as conceived, and probably experienced, by Ruysbroeck, can be divided into three great phases. We might call these Action, Reaction and Equilibrium. Broadly speaking, they answer to the Illumination, Dark Night and Simple Union of orthodox mystical science. Yet since in his vivid description of these linked states he constantly departs from the formulæ of his predecessors, and as constantly illustrates their statements by intimate and homely touches only possible to one who has endured the adventures of which he tells, we are justified in claiming the description as the fruit of experience rather than of tradition;

[1] *The Twelve Béguines*, cap. ix.

and as evidence of the course taken by his own development.

It is surely upon his own memory that he is relying, when he tells us that the beginning of this new life possesses something of the abrupt character of a second conversion. It happens, he says, when we least expect it; when the self, after the long tension and struggle of moral purgation, has become drowsy and tired. Then, suddenly, "a spiritual cry echoes through the soul," announcing a new encounter with Reality, and demanding a new response; or, to put it in another way, consciousness on its ascending spiral has pushed through to another level of existence, where it can hear voices and discern visions to which it was deaf and blind before. This sudden clarity of mind, this new vivid apprehension of Divine Love, is the first indication of man's entrance on the Illuminative Way. It is introversive rather than out-going in type. Changing the character of our attention to life, we discern within us something which we have always possessed and always ignored: a secret Divine energy, which is now to emerge from the subconscious deeps into the area of consciousness. There it stimulates the will, evicts all lesser images and interests from the heart, and concentrates all the faculties into a single and intense state, pressing towards the Unity of God, the synthetic experience of love; for perpetual movement towards that unity—not achievement of it—is the mark of this Second Life, in which the separation of God and the soul remains intact. In Victorine language, it is the period of spiritual betrothal, not of spiritual marriage; of a vision which, though wide, rich and wonderful, is mirrored rather than direct.

The new God-inspired movement, then, begins within, like a spring bubbling from the deeps; and thrusts up and out to the consciousness which it is destined to clarify and enhance. "The stream of Divine grace swiftly stirs and moves a man inwardly, and from within outwards; and this swift stirring is the first thing that makes us *see*. Of this swift stirring is born from the side of man the second point: that is, a gathering together of all the inward and outward powers in spiritual unity and in the bonds of love. The third is that liberty which enables man to retreat into himself, without images or obstacles, whensoever he wills and thinks of his God."[1]

So we may say that an enhancement of the conative powers, a greater control over the attention, are the chief marks of the Illuminative Way as perceived by the growing self. But the liberty here spoken of has

[1] *The Spiritual Marriage*, lib. ii. cap. iv.

a moral as well as a mental aspect. It is a freeing of the whole man from the fetters of illusion, and involves that perfect detachment of heart, that self-naughting, which makes him equally willing to have joy or pain, gain or loss, esteem or contempt, peace or fear, as the Divine Will may ordain. Thus is perfected that suppleness of soul which he began to acquire in the Active Life : a gradual process, which needs for its accomplishment the negative rhythm of renunciation, testing the manliness and courage of the self, as well as the positive movement of love. Hence the Contemplative Life, as Ruysbroeck knows and describes it, has, and must have, its state of pain as well as its state of joy. With him, however, as with nearly all the mystics, the state of joy comes first : the glad and eager reaction to those new levels of spiritual reality disclosed to consciousness when the struggles and readjustments of the Active Life have done their work. This is the phase in the self's progress which mystical writers properly mean by Illumination : a condition of great happiness, and of an intuition of Reality so vivid and joyous, that the soul often supposes that she has here reached the goal of her quest. It is in the spiritual year, says Ruysbroeck, that which the month of May is in the seasons of the earth ; a wholesome and necessary time

THE INTERIOR LIFE

of sunshine, swift growth and abundant flowers, when the soul, under the influence of ' the soft rain of inward consolations and the heavenly dew of the Divine sweetness ' blossoms in new and lovely graces.

Illumination is an unstable period. The sun is rising swiftly in the heaven of man's consciousness ; and as it increases in power, so it calls forth on the soul's part greater ardours, more intense emotional reactions. Once more the flux of God is demanding its reflux. The soul, like the growing boy suddenly made aware of the beauty, romance and wonder — the intense and irresistible appeal—of a world that had seemed ordinary before, flows out towards this new universe with all the enthusiasm and eagerness of its young fresh powers. Those powers are so new to it, that it cannot yet control or understand them. Vigorous and ungovernable, they invade by turns the heart, the will, the mind, as do the fevers and joys of physical adolescence ; inciting to acts and satisfactions for which the whole self is hardly ready yet. " Then is thrown wide," says Ruysbroeck, " the heaven which was shut, and from the face of Divine Love there blazes down a sudden light, as it were a lightning flash." In the meeting of this inward and outward spiritual force—the Divine Light without, the growing Divine Spark within—there is great joy. Ecstasy, and that state of musical rapture, exceeding the possibilities of speech, which Ruysbroeck like Richard Rolle calls 'ghostly song,' are the natural self-expressions of the soul in this moment of its career.[1]

In more than one book we find references to this ecstatic period : a period so strongly marked in his own case, that it became for him—though he was under no illusions as to its permanent value—one of the landmarks in man's journey to his home. Looking back on it in later life, he sees in it two great phases, of which the earlier and lower at any rate is dangerous and easily misunderstood ; and is concerned to warn those who come after him of its transitory and imperfect character. The first phase is that of 'spiritual inebriation,' in which the fever, excitement and unrest of this period of growth and change—affecting as they do every aspect of personality—show themselves in the psycho-physical phenomena which are well-known accompaniments of religious emotion in selves of a certain temperament. This spiritual delirium, which appears to have been a common phase in the mystical revivals of the fourteenth century, is viewed by Ruysbroeck with considerable distrust ; and rightly attributed by him to an excitement

[1] Cf. *The Twelve Béguines*, cap. x.

of the senses rather than of the soul. At best it is but 'children's food,' given to those who cannot yet digest 'the strong food of temptation and the loss of God.' Its manifestations, as he describes them, overpass the limits not merely of common sense but also of sanity; and are clearly related to the frenzies of revivalists and the wild outbreaks of songs, dance and ecstatic speech observed in nearly all non-Christian religions of an enthusiastic type. In this state of rapture, "a man seems like a drunkard, no longer master of himself." He sings, shouts, laughs and cries both at once, runs and leaps in the air, claps his hands, and indulges in absurdly exaggerated gestures 'with many other disagreeable exhibitions.'[1] These he may not be able to help; but is advised to control them as soon as he can, passing from the merely sensuous emotion which results when the light of Eternal Love invades the 'inferior powers' of the soul, to the spiritual emotion, amenable to reason, which is the reaction of the 'higher powers' of the self to that same overwhelming influx of grace.

That inpouring grace grows swiftly in power, as the strength of the sun grows with the passing of the year. The Presence of God now stands over the soul's supreme

[1] *The Spiritual Marriage*, lib. ii. cap. xix.; *The Book of Truth*, cap. ix.

summits, in the zenith : the transcendent fact of the illuminated consciousness. His power and love shine perpetually upon the heart, 'giving more than we can take, demanding more than we can pay'; and inducing in the soul upon which this mighty energy is playing, a strange unrest, part anguish and part joy. This is the second phase of the ecstatic period, and gives rise to that which Ruysbroeck, and after him Tauler, have called the 'storm of love': a wild longing for union which stretches to the utmost the self's powers of response, and expresses itself in violent efforts, impassioned ascents towards the Spirit that cries without ceasing to our spirit : " Pay your debt ! Love the Love that has loved you from Eternity." [1]

Now the vigorous soul begins to find within itself the gift of Spiritual Strength ; that enthusiastic energy which is one of the characters of all true love. This is the third of the 'Seven Gifts of the Spirit,' and the first to be actualised in the Illuminated Life.[2] From this strong and ardent passion for the Transcendent, adoration and prayer stream forth ; and these again react upon the self, forming the fuel of the fire of love. The interior invitation of God, His attractive power, His delicate yet in-

---

[1] *The Seven Degrees of Love,* cap. xiv.
[2] *The Kingdom of God's Lovers,* cap. xx.

exorable caress, is to the loving heart the most pure delight that it has ever known. It responds by passionate movements of adoration and gratitude, opening its petals wide to the beams of the Eternal Sun.

This is the joy; and close behind it comes the anguish, ' sweetest and heaviest of all pains.' It is the sense of unsatisfied desire — the pain of love — which comes from the enduring consciousness of a gulf fixed between the self and That with which it desires to unite. "Of this inward demand and compulsion, which makes the creature to rise up and prepare itself to the utmost of its power, without yet being able to reach or attain the Unity—of this, there springs a spiritual pain. When the heart's core, the very source of life, is wounded by love, and man cannot attain that thing which he desires above else; when he must stay ever where he desires no more to be, of these feelings comes this pain. . . . When man cannot achieve God, and yet neither can nor will do without Him; in such men there arises a furious agitation and impatience, both within and without. And whilst man is in this tumult, no creature in heaven or earth can help him or give him rest." [1]

The sensible heat of love is felt with a greater violence now than at any other period

[1] *The Spiritual Marriage*, lib. ii. cap. xxiii.

of life ; the rays of the Spiritual Sun strike the soul with terrific force, ripening the fruits of the virtues, yet bringing danger to the health, both mental and physical, of those who are not properly prepared, and who faint under the exhaustion of this 'intense fury of Divine Love,' this onslaught which 'eats up the heart.' These are 'the dog-days of the spiritual year.' As all nature languishes under their stifling heat, so too long an exposure to their violence may mean ruin to the physical health of the growing self. Yet those who behave with prudence need not take permanent harm ; a kind of wise steadfastness will support them throughout this turbulent period. "Following through all storms the path of love, they will advance towards that place whither love leadeth them."[1]

To this period of vivid illumination and emotional unrest belongs the development of those 'secondary automatisms' familiar to all students of mysticism : the desperate efforts of the mind to work up into some intelligible shape—some pictured vision or some spoken word—the overwhelming intuitions of the Transcendent by which it is possessed ; the abrupt suspension of the surface-consciousness in rapture and ecstasy, when that overwhelming intuition develops into the complete monoideism of the ecstatic,

[1] *Op. cit.*, lib. ii. cap. xxvii.

and cuts off all contacts with the world of sense. Of these phenomena Ruysbroeck speaks with intimacy, and also with much common sense. He distinguishes visions into those pictures or material images which are 'seen in the imagination,' and those so-called 'intellectual visions,'—of which the works of Angela of Foligno and St. Teresa provide so rich a series of examples,— which are really direct and imageless messages from the Transcendent; received in those supersensuous regions where man has contact with the Incomprehensible Good and "seeing and hearing are one thing." To this conventional classification he adds a passage which must surely be descriptive of his own experiences in this kind:

"Sometimes God gives to such men swift spiritual glimpses, like to the flash of lightning in the sky. It comes like a sudden flash of strange light, streaming forth from the Simple Nudity. By this is the spirit uplifted for an instant above itself; and at once the light passes, and the man again comes to himself. This is God's own work, and it is something most august; for often those who experience it afterwards become illuminated men. And those who live in the violence and fervour of love have now and then another manner, whereby a certain light shines *in* them; and this God works by means. In this light, the heart and the desirous powers are uplifted toward the Light; and in this encounter the joy and satisfaction are such that the heart cannot contain itself, but breaks out in loud cries of joy. And this is called *jubilus* or jubilation; and it is a joy that cannot be expressed in words." [1]

Here the parallel with Richard Rolle's ' ghostly song, with great voice outbreaking ' will strike every reader of that most musical of the mystics; and it is probable that in both cases the prominence given to this rather uncommon form of spiritual rapture points back to personal experience. "Methinketh," says Rolle, "that contemplation is this heavenly song of the Love of God, which is called *jubilus*, taken of the sweetness of a soul by praising of God. This song is the end of perfect prayer, and of the highest devotion that may be here. This gladness of soul is had of God, and it breaketh out in a ghostly voice well-sounding." [2]

This exultant and lyrical mood then, this adoring rapture, which only the rhythm of music can express, is the emotional reaction which indicates the high summer of the soul. It will be seen that each phase

[1] *The Spiritual Marriage*, lib. ii. cap. xxiv.
[2] Richard Rolle, *The Mending of Life*, cap. xii. (Harford's edition, p. 82).

of its seasonal progress has been marked by a fresh inflow of grace and gifts, a fresh demand upon its power of response. The tension never slackens; the need for industry is never done away. The gift of Strength, by which the self presses forward, has now been reinforced by the gift of Counsel, *i.e.* by the growth and deepening of that intuition which is its medium of contact with the spiritual world. The Counsel of the Spirit, says Ruysbroeck, is like a stirring or inspiration, deep within the soul. This stirring, this fresh uprush of energy, is really a ' new birth ' of the Son, the Divine Wisdom; lighting up the intelligence so that it perceives its destiny, and perceives too that the communion it now enjoys is but an image of the Divine Union which awaits it.[1] God is counselling the soul with an inward secret insistence to rush out towards Him, stimulating her hunger for Reality; or, to put it otherwise, the Divine Spark is growing swiftly, and pressing hard against the walls of its home. Therefore the culmination of this gift, and the culmination too of the illuminated consciousness, brings to the soul a certitude that she must still press on and out; that nothing less than God Himself can suffice her, or match the mysterious Thing which dwells in her deeps.

[1] *The Kingdom of God's Lovers*, cap. xxv.

Now this way of love and ecstasy and summer heats has been attended throughout by grave dangers for the adolescent spirit; above all by the primary danger which besets the mystical life, of mistaking spiritual joy for spiritual reality, desiring 'consolations' and 'illuminations' for their own sake, and resting in the gift instead of the Giver. "Though he who dedicates himself to love ever experiences great joy, he must never seek this joy." All those tendencies grouped by St. John of the Cross under the disagreeable name of 'spiritual gluttony,' those further temptations to self-indulgent quietism which are but an insidious form of sloth, are waiting to entrap the self on the Illuminative Way. But there is a way beyond this, another 'Coming of the Bridegroom,' which Ruysbroeck describes as 'eternally safe and sure.' This is the way of pain and deprivation; when the Presence of God seems to be withdrawn, and the fatigue and reaction consequent on the violent passions and energies of the illuminated state make themselves felt as a condition of misery, aridity and impotence,—all, in fact, that the Christian mystics mean by the 'Spiritual Death' or 'Dark Night of the Soul,' and which Ruysbroeck's contemporaries, the Friends of God, called 'the upper school of perfect self-abandonment.'

The mirror is now to be cleansed of all false reflections, all beautiful prismatic light; the thoughts stripped bare of the consolations they have enjoyed. Summer is over, and autumn begins; when the flowers indeed die down, but the fruits which they heralded are ripe. Now is the time when man can prove the stuff of which he is made; and the religious amorist, the false mystic, is distinguished from the heroic and long-suffering servant of God. " In this season is perfected and completed all the work that the sun has accomplished during the year. In the same manner, when Christ the glorious Sun has risen to His zenith in the heart of man and then begins to descend, and to hide the radiance of His Divine light, and to abandon the man; then the impatience and ardour of love grow less. And this concealment of Christ, and this withdrawal of His light and heat, are the first working and the new coming of this degree. And now Christ says spiritually within the man: 'Go forth, in the way which I now teach you.' And the man goes forth, and finds himself poor, wretched and abandoned. And here the tempest, the ardour, the impatience of love grows cold; and the hot summer becomes autumn, and its riches turn to great poverty. Then man begins to lament in his distress—where now has gone that ardent love, that intimacy, that gratitude, that all-sufficing adoration? And that interior consolation, that intimate joy, that sensible savour, how has he lost all this?"[1]

The veil that had seemed so transparent now thickens again; the certitudes that made life lovely all depart. Small wonder if the tortured spirit of the mystic fails to recognise this awful destitution as a renewed caress from the all-demanding Lover of the Soul; an education in courage, humility and selflessness; a last purification of the will. The state to which that self is being led is a renewed self-donation on new and higher levels: one more of those mystical deaths which are really mystical births; a giving-up, not merely of those natural tastes and desires which were disciplined in the Active Life, but of the higher passions and satisfactions of the spirit too. He is to be led to a state of such complete surrender to the Divine purposes that he is able to say: "Lord, not my will according to nature, but Thy will and my will according to spirit be done." The darkness, sorrow and abandonment through which this is accomplished are far more essential to his development than the sunshine and happiness that went before. It is not necessary, says Ruysbroeck, that all should know the ecstasies of illumination; but by this dark

[1] *The Spiritual Marriage*, lib. ii. cap. xxviii.

stairway every man who would attain to God must go.

When man has achieved this perfect resignation and all tendency to spiritual self-seeking is dead, the September of the soul is come. The sun has entered the sign of the Balance, when days and nights are equal; for now the surrendered self has achieved equilibrium, and endures in peace and steadfastness the alternations of the Divine Dark and Divine Light. Now the harvest and the vintage are ripe: " That is to say, all those inward and outward virtues, which man has practised with delight in the fire of love, these, now that he knows them and is able to accomplish them, he shall practise diligently and dutifully and offer them to God. And never were they so precious in His sight: never so noble and so fair. And all those consolations which God gave him before, he will gladly give up, and will empty himself for the glory of God. This is the harvest of the wheat and the many ripe fruits which make us rich in God, and give to us Eternal Life. Thus are the virtues perfected; and the absence of consolation is turned to an eternal wine." [1]

[1] *The Spiritual Marriage*, lib. ii. cap. xxix.

CHAPTER VII

THE INTERIOR LIFE: UNION AND CONTEMPLATION

Lume è lassu, che visibile face
lo Creatore a quella creatura
che solo in lui vedere ha la sua pace.
                                      PAR. XXX. 100.

And the Light floweth forth in similitude, and indraweth Itself in unity; which we perceive, beyond the reason, in that high point of our understanding which is bare and turned within.   THE TWELVE BÉGUINES.

THE soul which has endured with courage and humility the anguish of the Dark Night, actualising within its own experience the double rhythm of love and renunciation, now enters upon a condition of equilibrium; in which it perceives that all its previous adventures and apprehensions were but episodes of growth, phases in the long preparation of character for those new levels of life on which it is now to dwell.

Three points, says Ruysbroeck, must characterise the truly interior man. First, his mind must be detached from its natural inclination to rest in images and appearances, however lovely; and must depend altogether upon that naked Absence of Images, which is God. This is the 'ascent to the Nought' preached by the Areopagite. Secondly, by means of his spiritual exercises, his progressive efforts to correspond with that Divine Life ever experienced by him with greater intensity, he must have freed himself from all taint of selfhood, all personal desire; so that in true inward liberty he can lift himself up unhindered towards God, in a spirit of selfless devotion. Plainly, the desolations of the Dark Night are exactly adapted to the production within the self of these two characters; which we might call purity of intelligence and purity of will. Directly resulting from their actualisation, springs the third point: the consciousness of inward union with God.[1] This consciousness of union, which we must carefully distinguish from the *Unity* that is Ruysbroeck's name for the last state of the transfigured soul, is the ruling character of that state of equilibrium to which we have now come; and represents the full achievement of the Interior Life.

In many of his works, under various images, Ruysbroeck tries to tell us what he

[1] *The Sparkling Stone*, cap. ii.

means by this inward union with God, this 'mutual inhabitation,' as he calls it in one passage of great beauty, which is the goal of the 'Second Life.' He reminds us again of that remote point of the spirit, that 'apex' of our being, where our life touches the Divine Life; where God's image 'lives and reigns.' With the cleansing of the heart and mind, the heightening and concentration of the will, which the disciplines of the Active Life and Dark Night have effected, this supreme point of the spirit is brought at last within the conscious field. Then man feels and knows the presence there of an intense and creative vitality, an Eternal Essence, from which all that is worth having in his selfhood flows. This is the Life-giving Life (*Levende Leven*), where the created and Uncreated meet and are one: a phrase, apparently taken by Ruysbroeck from St. Bernard, which aptly expresses an idea familiar to all the great contemplatives. It is the point at which man's separate spirit, as it were, emerges from the Divine Spirit: the point through which he must at last return to his Source. Here the Father has impressed His image, the Son is perpetually born, the Spirit wells up;[1] and here the Divine Unity dwells and calls him to the One. Here Eternity and Time are intertwined. Here springs the

[1] Cp. *The Spiritual Marriage*, lib. ii. cap. lvii.

fountain of 'Living Water'—grace, transcendent vitality—upon which the mystic life of man depends.

Now the self, because it is at last conformed to the demands of the spiritual world, feels new powers from this life-giving source streaming into all departments of its being. The last barriers of self-will are broken; and the result is an inrush of fresh energy and light. Whereas in the 'First Life' God fed and communed with him by 'means,' and was revealed under images appropriate to a consciousness still immersed in the world of appearance; now man receives these gifts and messages, makes his contacts with Reality, 'without means,' or 'by grace'—*i.e.* in a spiritual and interior manner. Those 'lightning flashes from the face of Divine Love,' those abrupt and vivid intuitions which he enjoyed during illumination, have given way before the steady shining of the Uncreated Light. Though light-imagery is never long absent from Ruysbroeck's pages, it is, however, the spring of Living Water ever welling up, the rills or brooks which flow from it, and take its substance to the farthest recesses of the thirsty land, which seems to him the best image of this new inpouring of life. He uses it in all his chief works, perhaps most successfully in *The Spiritual Marriage*. Faithful to the mediæval division of personality into Memory or Mind, Intelligence or Understanding, and Will,—influenced too by his deep conviction that all Divine activity is threefold in type,—he describes the Wellspring as breaking into three Brooks of Grace, which pour their waters into each department of the self. The duct through which these waters come, 'living and foaming' from the deeps of the Divine Riches, is the Eternal Christ; who 'comes anew' to the purified soul, and is the immediate source of its power and happiness.

The first of the brooks which flow from Him is called 'Pure Simplicity.' It is a 'simple light,' says Ruysbroeck in another place; the white radiance of Eternity which, streaming into the mind, penetrates consciousness from top to bottom, and unifies the powers of the self about the new and higher centre now established. This simple light, in which we see things as they are—and therefore see that only one thing truly *is*—delivers us from that slavery to the multiplicity of things, which splits the attention and makes concentration upon Reality impossible to the soul. The achievement of such mental simplicity, escaping the prismatic illusion of the world, is the first condition of contemplation. "Thanks to this simple light which fills him, the man finds himself to be unified, established, penetrated and affirmed in the unity of his mind or thought. And thereby he is uplifted and established in a *new condition;* and he turns inward upon himself, and stays his mind upon the Nudity, above all the pressure of sensual images, above all multiplicity." [1]

The second stream which pours out from that Transcendent Life is a 'Spiritual Clarity,' which illuminates the intelligence and shows it all good. This clarity is a new and heightened form of intuition: a lucid understanding, whereby the self achieves clear vision of its own life, and is able to contemplate the sublime richness of the Divine Nature; gazing upon the mystery of the Trinity, and finding everywhere the Presence of God. Those who possess this light do not need ecstasies and revelations —sudden uprushes towards the supernal world—for their life and being is established in that world, above the life of sense. They have come to that state which Eckhart calls 'finding all creatures in God and God in all creatures.' They see things at last in their native purity. The heart of that vision, says Ruysbroeck, is their perception of "the unmeasured loyalty of God to His creation"—one of his deepest and most beautiful utterances—" and therefrom springs a deep inward joy of the spirit, and

[1] *The Spiritual Marriage*, lib. ii. cap. xxxvi.

a high trust in God ; and this inward joy embraces and penetrates all the powers of the soul, and the most secret part of the spirit." [1]

The third Brook of Grace irrigates the conative powers of the self ; strengthens the will in all perfection, and energises us anew. " Like fire, this brook enkindles the will, and swallows up and absorbs all things in the unity of the spirit . . . and now Christ speaks inwardly in the spirit by means of this burning brook, saying, ' Go forth, in exercises proper to this gift and this coming.' By the first brook, which is a *Simple Light*, the Mind is freed from the invasions of the senses, and grounded and affirmed in spiritual unity. And by the second brook, which is a *Spreading Light*, the Reason and Understanding are illuminated, that they may know and distinguish all manner of virtues and exercises, and the mysteries of Scripture. And by the third brook, which is an *Infused Heat*, the heights of the Will are enkindled with quiet love and adorned with great riches. And thus does man become spiritually illuminate ; for the grace of God dwells like a fountain-head in the unity of his spirit, and the brooks cause a flowing forth of all virtues from the powers of the soul. And the fountain-head of grace demands a back-

[1] *The Spiritual Marriage*, lib. ii. cap. xxxviii.

THE INTERIOR LIFE

flowing into that same ground from whence the flood has come."[1]

So the Interior Life, now firmly established, is found to conform to those great laws which have guided the growing spirit from the first. Again, the dual property of love, possession and action, satisfaction and fecundity, is to be manifested upon new levels. The pendulum motion of life, swinging between the experience of union with God to which 'the Divine Unity ever calls us,' and its expression in active charity to which the multiplicity of His creatures and their needs ever entreat us, still goes on. The more richly and strongly the life-giving Life wells up within the self, the greater are the demands made upon that self's industry and love. In the establishment of this balance, in this continual healthy act of alternation, this double movement into God and out to men, is the proof that the soul has really centred itself upon the spiritual world—is, as Ruysbroeck puts it, confirmed in love. "Thus do work and union perpetually renew themselves; and this renewal in work and in union, *this* is a spiritual life."[2]

Now the self which has achieved this degree of transcendence has achieved, too, considerable experience in that art of con-

[1] *The Spiritual Marriage*, lib. ii. cap. xxxix.
[2] *The Sparkling Stone*, cap. ii.

templation or introversion which is the mode of its communion with God. Throughout, training and development have gone hand in hand; and the fact that Ruysbroeck seldom troubles to distinguish between them, but accepts them as two aspects of one thing—the gradual deification of the soul—constitutes one of the great obstacles to an understanding of his works. Often he describes the whole spiritual life as consisting in introversion, an entering of consciousness into the supersensuous regions beyond thought; in defiance of his own principle of active charity, movement, work, as the essential reaction to the universe which distinguishes a 'deified' man. The truth is that the two processes run side by side; and now one, now the other, is in the foreground of his thought. Therefore all that I shall now say of the contemplative art must be understood as describing acts and apprehensions taking place throughout the whole course of the Interior Life.

What, then, is introversion? It is one of the two great modes under which the spiritual consciousness works. Plainly, any living sense of God's presence must discern that Circle whose centre is everywhere, as both exterior and interior to the self. In Ruysbroeck's own works we find a violent effort to express this ineffable fact of omnipresence, of a truly Transcendent yet truly Immanent Reality; an effort often involving a collision of imagery. God, he says, may be discovered at the soul's apex, where He 'eternally lives and reigns'; and the soul itself dwells *in* God, ebbing and flowing, wandering and returning, within that Fathomless Ground. Yet none the less He comes to that soul from without; pouring in upon it like sunshine, inundating it with torrents of grace, seizing the separate entity and devouring whilst He feeds it; flashing out upon it in a tempest of love from the Empyrean Heaven, the Abyss of Being, where He dwells. "Present, yet absent; near, yet far!" exclaims St. Augustine. "Thou art the sky, and Thou art the nest as well!" says the great mystic poet of our own day.

Whilst nearly all the mystics have possessed clear consciousness of this twofold revelation of the Divine Nature, and some have experienced by turns the 'outward and upward' rush and the inward retreat, temperamentally they usually lean towards one or other form of communion with God, —ecstasy or introversion. For one class, contact with Him seems primarily to involve an outgoing flight towards Transcendent Reality; an attitude of mind strongly marked in all contemplatives who are near to the Neoplatonic tradition — Plotinus,

St. Basil, St. Macarius—and also in Richard Rolle and a few other mediæval types. These would agree with Dionysius the Areopagite that "we must contemplate things divine by our whole selves standing *out* of our whole selves." For the other class, the first necessity is a retreat of consciousness from the periphery, where it touches the world of appearance, to the centre, the Unity of Spirit or 'Ground of the Soul,' where human personality buds forth from the Essential World. True, this inturning of attention is but a preliminary to the self's entrance upon that same Transcendent Region which the ecstatic claims that he touches in his upward flights. The introversive mystic, too, is destined to 'sail the wild billows of the Sea Divine'; but here, in the deeps of his nature, he finds the door through which he must pass. Only by thus discovering the unity of his own nature can he give himself to that 'tide of light' which draws all things back to the One.

Such is Ruysbroeck's view of contemplation. This being so, introversion is for him an essential part of man's spiritual development. As the Son knows the Father, so it is the destiny of all spirits created in that Pattern to know Him; and the mirror which is able to reflect that Divine Light, the Simple Eye which alone

can bear to gaze on it, lies in the deeps
of human personality. The will, usually
harnessed to the surface-consciousness, devoted to the interests of temporal life ; the
love, so freely spent on unreal and imperfect objects of desire ; the thought which
busies itself on the ceaseless analysis and
arrangement of passing things—all these
are to be swept inwards to that gathering-
point of personality, that Unity of the
Spirit, of which he so often speaks ; and
there fused into a single state of enormously
enhanced consciousness, which, withdrawn
from all attention to the changeful world
of ' similitudes,' is exposed to the direct
action of the Eternal World of spiritual
realities. The pull of Divine Love — the
light that ever flows back into the One—
is to withdraw the contemplative's consciousness from multiplicity to unity. His
progress in contemplation will be a progress
towards that complete mono-ideism in
which the Vision of God—and here *vision*
is to be understood in its deepest sense as a
totality of apprehension, a ' ghostly sight '—
dominates the field of consciousness to the
exclusion, for the time of contemplation,
of all else.

Psychologically, Ruysbroeck's method
differs little from that described by St.
Teresa. It begins in recollection, the first
drawing inwards of attention from the

world of sense; passes to meditation, the centring of attention on some intellectual formula or mystery of faith; and thence, by way of graduated states, variously divided and described in his different works, to contemplation proper, the apprehension of God 'beyond and above reason.' All attempts, however, to map out this process, or reduce it to a system, must necessarily have an arbitrary and symbolic character. True, we are bound to adopt some system, if we describe it at all; but the dangers and limitations of all formulas, all concrete imagery, where we are dealing with the fluid, living, changeful world of spirit, should never be absent from our minds. The bewildering and often inconsistent series of images and numbers, arrangements and rearrangements of 'degrees,' 'states,' 'stirrings,' and 'gifts,' in which Ruysbroeck's sublime teachings on contemplation are buried, makes the choice of some one formula imperative for us; though none will reduce his doctrines to a logical series, for he is perpetually passing over from the dialectic to the lyrical mood, and forgets to be orderly as soon as he begins to be subjective. I choose, then, to base my classification on that great chapter (xix.) in *The Seven Cloisters*, where he distinguishes three stages of contemplation; finding in them the responses of consciousness to the special action of the Three Persons of the Blessed Trinity. These three stages in the soul's apprehension of God, are: the Emotional, the Intellectual, the Intuitive. I think that most of the subtly distinguished interior experiences of the mystic, the ' comings ' of the Divine Presence, the ' stirrings ' and contacts which he describes in his various books, can be ranged under one or other of them.

1. First comes that loving contemplation of the ' uplifted heart ' which is the work of the Holy Spirit, the consuming fire of Divine Love. This ardent love, invading the self, and satisfying it in that intimate experience of personal communion so often described in the writings of the mystics, represents the self's first call to contemplation and first natural response; made with " so great a joy and delight of soul and body, in his uplifted heart, that the man knoweth not what hath befallen him, nor how he may endure it." For Ruysbroeck this purely emotional reaction to Reality, this burning flame of devotion — which seemed to Richard Rolle the essence of the contemplative life—is but its initial phase. It corresponds with—and indeed generally accompanies — those fever - heats, those ' tempests ' of impatient love endured by the soul at the height of the Illuminative Way. Love, it is true, shall be from first to last

the inspiring force of the contemplative's ascents : his education is from one point of view simply an education in love. But this love is a passion of many degrees; and the 'urgency felt in the heart,' the restlessness and hunger of this spiritual feeling-state, is only its lowest form. The love which burns like white fire on the apex of the soul, longs for sacrifice, inspires heroic action, and goes forward without fear, 'holy, strong and free,' to brave the terrors of the Divine Dark, is of another temper than this joyful sentiment.

2. A loving stretching out into God, and an intellectual gazing upon Him, says Ruysbroeck, in a passage which I have already quoted, are the 'two heavenly pipes' in which the wind of the Spirit sings. So the next phase in the contemplative's development is that enhancement of the intellect, the power of perceiving, as against desiring and loving Reality, which is the work of the Logos, the Divine Wisdom. As the cleansed and detached heart had been lifted up to *feel* the Transcendent; now the understanding, stripped of sense-images, purged of intellectual arrogance, clarified by grace, is lifted up to *apprehend* it. This degree has two phases. First, that enlargement of the understanding to an increased comprehension of truth, the finding of deeper and diviner meanings in things already

known, which Richard of St. Victor called *mentis dilatatio*. Next, that further uplift of the mind to a state in which it is able to contemplate things above itself whilst retaining clear self-consciousness, which he called *mentis sublevatio*. Ruysbroeck, however, inverts the order given by Richard; for him the uplift comes first, the dilation of consciousness follows from it. This is a characteristic instance of the way in which he uses the Victorine psychology; constantly appropriating its terms but never hesitating to modify, enrich or misuse them as his experience or opinions may dictate.

The first phase of Intellectual Contemplation, then, is a lifting of the mind to a swift and convincing vision of Reality: one of those sudden, incommunicable glimpses of Truth so often experienced early in the contemplative's career. The veil parts, and he sees a " light and vision, which give to the contemplating spirit a conscious certitude that she sees God, so far as man may see Him in mortal life."[1] That strange mystical light of which all contemplatives speak, and which Ruysbroeck describes in a passage of great subtlety as 'the intermediary between the seeing thought and God,' now floods his consciousness. In it "the Spirit of the Father speaks in the uplifted thought which is bare and stripped of

[1] *The Twelve Béguines*, cap. xi.

images, saying, 'Behold Me as I behold thee.' Then the pure and single eyes are strengthened by the inpouring of that clear Light of the Father, and they behold His face, in a simple vision, beyond reason, and without reason." [1]

It might be thought that in this 'simple vision' of Supreme Reality, the spirit of the contemplative reached its goal. It has, indeed, reached a point at which many a mystic stops short. I think, however, that a reference to St. Augustine, whose influence is so strongly marked in Ruysbroeck's works, will show what he means by this phase of contemplation; and the characters which distinguish it from that infused or unitive communion with God which alone he calls *Contemplatio*. In the seventh book of his *Confessions*, Augustine describes just such an experience as this. By a study of the books of the Platonists he had learned the art of introversion, and achieved by its aid a fleeting 'Intellectual Contemplation' of God; in his own words, a "hurried vision of That which Is." "Being by these books," he says, "admonished to return into myself, I entered into the secret closet of my soul, guided by Thee . . . and beheld the Light that never changes, above the eye of my soul, above the intelligence." [2] It was

[1] *Loc. cit.*
[2] St. Augustine, *Confessions*, lib. vii. cap. x.

THE INTERIOR LIFE

by "the withdrawal of thought from experience, its abstraction from the contradictory throng of sensuous images," that he attained to this transitory apprehension; which he describes elsewhere as "the *vision* of the Land of Peace, but not the *road* thereto." But intellect alone could not bear the direct impact of the terrible light of Reality; his "weak sight was dazzled by its splendour," he "could not sustain his gaze," and turned back to that humble discovery of the Divine Substance by means of Its images and attributes, which is proper to the intellectual power.[1]

Now surely this is the psychological situation described by Ruysbroeck. The very images used by Augustine are found again in him. The mind of the contemplative, purified, disciplined, deliberately abstracted from images, is inundated by the divine sunshine, "the Light which is not God, but that whereby we see Him"; and in this radiance achieves a hurried but convincing vision of Supreme Reality. But "even though the eagle, king of birds, can with his powerful sight gaze steadfastly upon the brightness of the sun; yet do the weaker eyes of the bat fail and falter in the same."[2] The intellectual vision is dazzled and distressed, like a man who can bear the diffused

[1] St. Augustine, *Confessions,* lib. vii. capp. xvii. and xx.
[2] *The Twelve Béguines,* cap. xii.

radiance of sunshine but is blinded if he dares to follow back its beams to the terrible beauty of their source. "Not for this are my wings fitted," says Dante, drooping to earth after his supreme ecstatic flight. Because it cannot sustain its gaze, then, the intelligence falls back upon the second phase of intellectual contemplation: *Speculatio*, the deep still brooding in which the soul, 'made wise by the Spirit of Truth,' contemplates God and Creation as He and it are reflected in the clear mirror of her intellectual powers, under 'images and similitudes'—the Mysteries of Faith, the Attributes of the Divine Nature, the forms and manners of created things. As the Father contemplates all things in the Son, 'Mirror of Deity,' so now does the introverted soul contemplate Him in this 'living mirror of her intelligence' on which His sunshine falls. Because her swift vision of That which Is has taught her to distinguish between the ineffable Reality and the Appearance which shadows it forth, she can again discover Him under those images which once veiled, but now reveal His presence. The intellect which has apprehended God Transcendent, if only for a moment, has received therefrom the power of discerning God Immanent. "He shows Himself to the soul in the living mirror of her intelligence; not as He is in His nature, but in images and similitudes, and in the degree in which the illuminated reason can grasp and understand Him. And the wise reason, enlightened of God, sees clearly and without error in images of the understanding all that she has heard of God, of faith, of truth, according to her longing. But that image which is God Himself, although it is held before her, she cannot comprehend; for the eyes of her understanding must fail before that Incomparable Light." [1]

In *The Kingdom of God's Lovers* Ruysbroeck pours forth a marvellous list of the attributes under which the illuminated intelligence now contemplates and worships That Which she can never comprehend; that "Simple One in whom all multitude and all that multiplies, finds its beginning and its end." From this simple Being of the Godhead the illuminated reason abstracts those images and attributes with which it can deal, as the lower reason abstracts from the temporal flux the materials of our normal universe. Such a loving consideration of God under His attributes is the essence of meditation: and meditation is in fact the way in which the intellectual faculties can best contemplate Reality. But "because all things, when they are considered in their inwardness, have their beginning and their ending in the Infinite

[1] *Loc. cit.*

Being as in an Abyss," here again the contemplative is soon led above himself and beyond himself, to a point at which intellect and 'consideration'—*i.e.* formal thought—fail him; because " here we touch the Simple Nature of God." When intellectual contemplation has brought the self to this point, it has done its work; for it has " excited in the soul an eager desire to lift itself up by contemplation into the simplicity of the Light, that thereby its avid desire of infinite fruition may be satisfied and fulfilled";[1] *i.e.* it has performed the true office of meditation, induced a shifting of consciousness to higher levels.

We observe that the emphasis, which in the First Degree of Contemplation fell wholly on feeling, in the Second Degree falls wholly upon knowledge. We are not, however, to suppose from this that emotion has been left behind. As the virtues and energies of the Active Life continue in the Contemplative Life, so the 'burning love' which distinguished the first stage of communion with the Transcendent, is throughout the source of that energy which presses the self on to deeper and closer correspondences with Reality. Its presence is presupposed in all that is said concerning the development of the spiritual consciousness. Nevertheless Ruysbroeck, though he cannot be

[1] *The Kingdom of God's Lovers*, cap. xxxiv.

accused of intellectualism, is led by his admiration for Victorine ideas to lay great stress upon the mental side of contemplation, as against those emotional reactions to the Transcendent which are emphasised—almost to excess—by so many of the saints. His aim was the lifting of the *whole man* to Eternal levels: and the clarifying of the intelligence, the enhancement of the understanding, seemed to him a proper part of the deification of human nature, the bringing forth in the soul's ground of that Son who is the Wisdom of God as well as the Pattern of Man. Though he moves amongst deep mysteries, and in regions beyond the span of ordinary minds, there is always apparent in him an effort towards lucidity of expression, sharp definition, plain speech. Sometimes he is wild and ecstatic, pouring forth his vision in a strange poetry which is at once uncouth and sublime; but he is never woolly or confused. His prose passages owe much of their seeming difficulty to the passion for exactitude which distinguishes and classifies the subtlest movements of the spiritual atmosphere, the delicately graded responses of the soul.

3. Now the Third Degree of Contemplation lifts the whole consciousness to a plane of perception which transcends the categories of the intellect: where it deals no longer with the label but with the Thing.

It has passed beyond image and also beyond
thought; to that knowledge by contact
which is the essence of intuition, and is
brought about by the higher powers of
love. Such contemplation is regarded by
Ruysbroeck as the work of the Father,
"Who strips from the mind all forms and
images and lifts up the Naked Apprehension [*i.e.* intuition] into its Origin, that is
Himself." [1] It is effected by concentration of all the powers of the self into a
single state 'uplifted above all action, in a
bare understanding and love,' upon that apex
of the soul where no reason can ever attain,
and where the ' simple eye ' is ever open
towards God. There the loving soul apprehends Him, not under conditions, 'in some
wise,' but as a *whole*, without the discrete
analysis of His properties which was the
special character of intellectual contemplation; a synthetic experience which is 'in
no wise.' This is for Ruysbroeck the contemplative act *par excellence*. It is 'an
intimacy which is ignorance,' a 'simple
seeing,' he says again and again; "and
the name thereof is *Contemplatio;* that is,
the seeing of God in simplicity." [2]

" Here the reason no less than all separate acts must give way, for our powers
become simple in Love; they are silent

[1] *The Seven Cloisters*, cap. xix.
[2] *The Twelve Béguines*, cap. xii.

and bowed down in the Presence of the Father. And this revelation of the Father lifts the soul above the reason into the Imageless Nudity. There the soul is simple, pure, spotless, empty of all things; and it is in this state of perfect emptiness that the Father manifests His Divine radiance. To this radiance neither reason nor sense, observation nor distinction, can attain. All this must stay below; for the measureless radiance blinds the eyes of the reason, they cannot bear the Incomprehensible Light. But above the reason, in the most secret part of the understanding, the *simple eye* is ever open. It contemplates and gazes at the Light with a pure sight that is lit by the Light itself: eye to eye, mirror to mirror, image to image. This threefold act makes us like God, and unites us to Him; for the sight of the *simple eye* is a living mirror, which God has made for His image, and whereon He has impressed it."[1]

Intuitive or infused contemplation is the form of communion with the Transcendent proper to those who have grown up to the state of Union; and feel and know the presence of God within the soul, as a love, a life, an 'indrawing attraction,' calling and enticing all things to the still unachieved consummation of the Divine Unity. He who has reached this pitch of introversion,

[1] *The Mirror of Eternal Salvation*, cap. xvii.

and is able, in his spiritual exercises, to withdraw himself thus to the most secret part of his spirit, feels—within the Eternal Light which fills his mirror and is 'united with it,'—this perpetual demand of the Divine Unity, entreating and urging him towards a total self-loss. In the fact that he knows this demand and impulsion as other than himself, we find the mark which separates this, the highest contemplation proper to the Life of Union, from that 'fruitive contemplation' of the spirit which has died into God which belongs to the Life of Unity.[1] When the work of transmutation is finished and he has received the 'Sparkling Stone of Divine Humanity,' this subject-object distinction — though really an eternal one, as Ruysbroeck continually reminds us—will no longer be possible to his consciousness. Then he will live at those levels to which he now makes impassioned ascents in his hours of unitive prayer: will be immersed in the Beatific Vision on which he now looks, and 'lose himself in the Imageless Nudity.'

This is the clue to the puzzling distinction made by Ruysbroeck between the contemplation which is 'without conditions,' and that which is 'beyond and above conditions' and belongs to the Superessential Life alone. In Intuitive Contemplation the

[1] *The Sparkling Stone*, cap. iii.

seeing self apprehends the Unconditioned World, *Onwise*, and makes 'loving ascents thereto.' It 'finds within itself the unwalled'; yet is still anchored to the conditioned sphere. In Superessential Contemplation, it *dies into* that 'world which is in no wise.' In the great chapter of *The Sparkling Stone*[1] where he struggles to make this distinction clear, Ruysbroeck says that the Friends of God (*i.e.* the Interior Men) "cannot with themselves and all their works penetrate to that Imageless Nudity." Although they feel united with God, yet they feel in that union an otherness and difference between themselves and God; and therefore "the ascent into the Nought is unknown to them." They feel themselves carried up towards God in the tide of His all-subduing Fire of Love; but they retain their selfhood, and may not be consumed and burned to nothing in the Unity of Love. They do not yet desire to die into God, that they may receive a deiform life from Him; but they are in the way which leads to this fulfilment of their destiny, and are "following back the light to its Origin."

This following-back is one continuous process, in which we, for convenience of description, have made artificial breaks.

[1] Cap. viii.: 'Of the Difference between the Secret Friends and the Hidden Sons of God.'

It is the thrust of consciousness deeper and deeper into the heart of Reality. As in the stream of physical duration, so in this ceaseless movement of the spirit, there is a persistence of the past in the present, a carrying through and merging of one state in the next. Thus the contemplation which is ' wayless,' the self's intuitive communion with the Infinite Life and Light, growing in depth and richness, bridges the gap which separates the Interior and the Superessential Life.

We find in Ruysbroeck's works indications of a transitional state, in which the soul " is guided and lost, wanders and returns, ebbs and flows," within the ' limitless Nudity,' to which it has not yet wholly surrendered itself. " And its seeing is in no wise, being without manner, and it is neither thus nor thus, neither here nor there; for that which is in no wise hath enveloped all, and the vision is made high and wide. It knows not itself where That is which it sees; and it cannot come thereto, for its seeing is in no wise, and passes on, beyond, for ever, and without return. That which it apprehends it cannot realise in full, nor wholly attain, for its apprehension is wayless, and without manner, and therefore it is apprehended of God in a higher way than it can apprehend Him. Behold! such a following of the Way that is Wayless, is intermediary between contemplation in images and similitudes of the intellect, and unveiled contemplation beyond all images in the Light of God." [1]

[1] *The Twelve Béguines*, cap. xii.

CHAPTER VIII

THE SUPERESSENTIAL LIFE

If, therefore, thou art become the throne of God and the Heavenly Charioteer hath seated Himself within thee, and thy soul is wholly become a spiritual eye and is wholly made into light; if, too, thou art nourished with the heavenly food of that Spirit and hast drunk of the Living Water and put on the secret vesture of light—if thine inward man has experienced all these things and is established in abundant faith, lo! thou livest indeed the Eternal Life and thy soul rests even in this present time with the Lord. St. Macarius of Egypt.

We have seen that Ruysbroeck, in common with a few other supreme mystics, declares to us as veritably known and experienced by him, a universe of three orders—Becoming, Being, God—and further, three ways of life whereby the self can correspond to these three orders, and which he calls the life of nature, the life of grace, the life of glory. 'Glory,' which has been degraded by the usage of popular piety into a vague superlative, and finally left in the hands of hymn-writers and religious revivalists, is one of the most ancient technical terms of Christian mysticism. Of Scriptural origin, from the fourth century to the fifteenth it was used to denote a definite kind of enhanced life, a final achievement of Reality—the unmediated radiance of God—which the gift of ' divine sonship ' made possible to the soul. In the life of grace, that soul transcends conditions in virtue of a Divine vitality poured in from the Absolute Sphere, and actualises its true being (*Wesen*); in the life of glory, it becomes a denizen of that sphere, and achieves an existence that is 'more than being' (*Overwesen*). The note of the first state is contemplation, awareness ; the note of the second is fruition, possession.

That power of making ' swift and loving ascents ' to the plane of *Onwise* to which man attained at the end of the Interior Life, that conscious harmony with the Divine Will which then became the controlling factor of his active career, cannot be the end of the process of transcendence. The soul now hungers and thirsts for a more intense Reality, a closer contact with ' Him who is measureless ' ; a deeper and deeper penetration into the burning heart of the universe. Though contemplation seems to have reached its term, love goes on, to ' lose itself upon the heights.' Beyond both the conditioned and unconditioned world, beyond the Trinity Itself, that love discerns its ultimate objective—the very Godhead, the Divine Unity, "where all lines find their end"; where "we are satisfied and overflowing, and with Him beyond ourselves eternally fulfilled."[1] The abiding life which is there discoverable, is not only 'without manner' but 'above manner'—the 'deified life,' indescribable save by the oblique methods of music or poetry, wherein, in Maeterlinck's great phrase, "the psychology of man mingles with the psychology of God." All Ruysbroeck's most wonderful passages are concerned with the desperate attempt to tell us of this 'life,' this utter fruition of Reality: which seems at one time to involve for the contemplative consciousness a self-mergence in Deity, so complete as to give colour to that charge of pantheism which is inevitably flung at all mystics who try to tell what they have known; at others, to represent rather the perfect consummation of that 'union in separateness' which is characteristic of all true love.

This is but one instance of that perpetual and inevitable resort to paradox which torments all who try to follow him along this 'track without shadow of trace'; for the goal towards which he is now enticing us is one in which all the completing opposites of our fragmentary experience find their

[1] *The Twelve Béguines*, cap. xvi.

bourne. Hence the rapid alternation of spatial and personal symbols which confuses our industrious intellects, is the one means whereby he can suggest its actuality to our hungry hearts.

As we observed in Ruysbroeck's earlier teaching on contemplation three distinct forms, in which the special work that theology attributes to the three Divine Persons seemed to him to be reflected; now, in this Superessential Contemplation, or Fruition, we find the work of the Absolute Godhead Itself, energising upon a plane of intensity which so utterly transcends our power of apprehension, that it seems to the surface consciousness — as Dionysius the Areopagite had named it — a negation of all things, a Divine Dark.

This Fruition, says Ruysbroeck, "is wild and desolate as a desert, and therein is to be found no way, no road, no track, no retreat, no measure, no beginning, no end, nor any other thing that can be told in words. And this is for all of us Simple Blessedness, the Essence of God and our superessence, above reason and beyond reason. To know it we must be in it, beyond the mind and above our created being; in that Eternal Point where all our lines begin and end, that Point where they lose their name and all distinction, and become one with the Point itself, and that very One which the Point is, yet nevertheless ever remain in themselves nought else but lines that come to an end." [1]

What, then, is the way by which the soul moves from that life of intense contemplation in which the 'spreading light' of the Spirit shows her the universe fulfilled with God, to this new transfigured state of joy and terror? It is a way for which her previous adventures might have prepared us. As each new ascent, new inflow of grace, was prepared by a time of destitution and stress —as the compensating beats of love and renunciation have governed the evolving melody of the inner life—so here a last death of selfhood, a surrender more absolute than all that has gone before, must be the means of her achievement of absolute life.

"Dying, and behold I live!" says Paul of his own attainment of supernal life in Christ. Ruysbroeck, who never strays far from the vital and heroic mysticism of the New Testament saints, can find no other language for this last crisis of the spirit—its movement from the state of *Wesen* to that of *Overwesen*—than the language of death. The ever-moving line, though its vital character of duration continues, now seems to itself to swoon into the Point; the separate entity which has felt the flood of grace pour into it to energise its active career, and the

[1] *The Seven Cloisters*, cap. xix.

ebb of homeward-tending love draw it back towards the One, now feels itself pouring into the Infinite Sea. Our personal activity, he says, has done all that it can: as the separate career of Christ our Pattern closed with His voluntary death, so the death of our selfhood on that apex of personality where we have stretched up so ardently toward the Father, shall close the separate career of the human soul and open the way to its new, God-driven career, its resurrection-life. "None is sure of Eternal Life unless he has died with all his own attributes wholly into God"[1]—all else falls short of the demands of supreme generosity.

It is *The Book of the Sparkling Stone* which contains Ruysbroeck's most wonderful descriptions of the consciousness peculiar to these souls who have grown up to 'the fulness of the stature of Christ'; and since this is surely the finest and perhaps the least known of his writings, I offer no apology for transcribing a long passage from its ninth chapter: 'How we may become the Hidden Sons of God.'

"When we soar up above ourselves, and become, in our upward striving towards God, so simple, that the naked Love in the Heights can lay hold on us, there where Love cherishes Love, above all activity and all virtue (that is to say, in our Origin,

[1] *The Sparkling Stone*, cap. viii.

wherefrom we are spiritually born)—then we cease, and we and all that is our own die into God. And in this death we become hidden Sons of God, and find in ourselves a new life, and that is Eternal Life. And of these Sons, St. Paul says : ' Ye are dead, and your life is hid with Christ in God.' In our approach to God we must bear with us ourselves and all that we do, as a perpetual sacrifice to God ; and in the Presence of God we must leave ourselves and all our works, and, dying in love, soar up above all created things into the Superessential Kingdom of God. And of this the Spirit of God speaks in the Book of Hidden Things, saying : ' Blessed are the dead that die in the Lord.' . . . If we would *taste* God, and feel in ourselves Eternal Life above all things, we must go forth into God with a faith that is far above our reason, and there dwell, simple, idle, without image, lifted up by love into the Unwalled Bareness of our intelligence. For when we go out from ourselves in love, and die to all observances in ignorance and darkness, then we are made complete, and transfigured by the Eternal Word, Image of the Father. And in this emptiness of spirit we receive the Incomprehensible Light, which enfolds and penetrates us as air is penetrated by the light of the sun ; and this Light is nought else but a fathomless gazing and seeing. What we are, that we

THE SUPERESSENTIAL LIFE

gaze at; and what we gaze at, that we are. For our thought, our life, our being, are lifted up in simplicity, and united with the Truth, that is God. Therefore in this simple gazing we are one life and one spirit with God—and this I call the *seeing life*."[1]

Such a passage as this lies beyond our poor attempts at analysis. Those only will understand it who yield themselves to it; entering into its current, as we enter into the music that we love. It tells us all it can of this life which is 'more than being,' as *felt* in the supreme experience of love. Life and Death, Dark and Light, Idleness, Bareness— these are but images of the feeling-states that accompany it. But here, more than elsewhere in Ruysbroeck's writings, we must remember the peril which goes with all subjective treatment of mystical truth. Each state which the unitive mystic experiences is so intense, that it monopolises for the time being his field of consciousness. Writing under the 'pressure of the Spirit' he writes of it—as indeed it seems to him at the moment—as ultimate and complete. Only by a comparison of different and superficially inconsistent descriptions of this enhanced life — which must harmonise and fulfil *all* the needs of our complex personality, providing inexhaustible objectives

[1] *The Sparkling Stone*, cap. ix.

for love, intelligence and will—can we form any true idea concerning it.

When we do this, we discover that the side of it which *seems* a static beatitude, still Fruition, perfect Rest, is always balanced by the other side; which *seems* a perpetual and progressive attainment, a seeking and finding, a hungering and feeding, a giving and taking. These coexist; as the ever-renewed 'coming of the Bridegroom,' the welling-up of the Spirit, the stormy, eager, unsatisfied love of the soul do as a matter of experience coexist within that perfect and personal union wherein Love and Fruition, as Ruysbroeck puts it, 'live between action and rest.' The alternate consciousness of the line and the Point, the moving river and the Sea, the relative and the Absolute, persists so long as consciousness persists at all; it is no Christianised Nirvana into which he seeks to induct us, but that mysterious synthesis of Being and Becoming, 'eternal stillness and eternal work'—a movement into God which is already a complete achievement of Him—which certain other great mystics have discerned beyond the 'flaming ramparts' of the common life.

The unbreakable unity with God, which constitutes the mark of the Third Life, exists in the 'essential ground of the soul'; where the river flows into the Sea, the line

THE SUPERESSENTIAL LIFE

into the Point; where the pendulum of self has its attachment to Reality. *There*, the hidden child of the Absolute is ' one with God in restful fruition '; there, his deep intuition of Divine things—that ' Savouring Wisdom ' which is the last supreme gift of the Spirit [1]— is able to taste and apprehend the sweetness of Infinite Reality. But at the other end, where he still participates in the time-process, where his love and will are a moving river, consciousness hungers for that total Attainment still; and attention will swing between these two extremes, now actualised within the living soul, which has put on the dual character of ' Divine Humanity ' and is living Eternal Life, not in some far-off celestial region, but here, where Christ lived it, in the entangled world of Time. Thus active self-mergence, incessant re-birth into God, perpetual eager feeding on Him, is implicit in all spiritual life. Even for the souls of the ' deified,' quietism is never right. " For love cannot be lazy, but would search through and through, and taste through and through, the fathomless kingdom that lives in her ground; and this hunger shall *never* be stilled." [2]

The soul, whenever it attends to itself—withdraws itself, so to speak, from the

---

[1] *The Kingdom of God's Lovers*, cap. xxxiii.
[2] *The Sparkling Stone*, cap. ix.; cp. also *The Twelve Béguines*, cap. xvi.

Divine Synthesis, dwells in itself, and beholds instead of being—feels again the 'eternal unrest of love'; the whip of the Heavenly Charioteer, driving all spirits in towards the heart of God, where they are 'one fire with Him.' "This stirring, that mediates between ourselves and God, we can never pass beyond; and what that stirring is in its essence, and what love is in itself, we can never know."[1] But when it dwells beyond itself, and in the supreme moments of ecstasy merges its consciousness in the Universal Consciousness, it transcends succession and centres itself in the Divine Selfhood—the 'still, glorious, and absolute One-ness.' Then it feels, not hunger but satisfaction, not desire but fruition; and knows itself beyond reason 'one with the abysmal depth and breadth,' in "a simple fathomless savouring of all good and of Eternal Life. And in this savouring we are swallowed up, above reason and beyond reason, in the deep Quiet of the Godhead which is never moved."[2]

Such experiences however, such perfect fruition, in which the self dies into the overwhelming revelation of the Transcendent, and its rhythm is merged in the Divine Rhythm, cannot be continuous for

[1] *The Twelve Béguines*, cap. xvi.
[2] *The Sparkling Stone*, cap. ix.; cp. also *The Book of Truth*, cap. xii.

those still living in the flesh. There is in Ruysbroeck no foolish insistence on any impossible career of ceaseless ecstasy; but a robust acceptance of the facts and limitations of life. Man cannot, he says, " perpetually contemplate with attention the superessential Being of God in the Light of God. But whosoever has attained to the gift of Intelligence [*i.e.* the sixth of the Seven Gifts of the Spirit] attains this power, which becomes habitual to him; and whensoever he will, he can wholly absorb himself in this manner of contemplation, in so far as it is possible in this life." [1]

The superessential man, in fact, is, as Francis Thompson said of the soul, a

> ". . . swinging-wicket set
> Between
> The Unseen and Seen."

He is to move easily and at will between these two orders, both actual, both God-inhabited, the complementary expressions of One Love; participating both in the active, industrious, creative outflow in differentiation, and the still indrawing attraction which issues in the supreme experience of Unity. For these two movements the Active and Interior Lives have educated him. The truly characteristic experience of the Third Life is the fruition of that Unity

[1] *The Kingdom of God's Lovers*, cap. xxxi.

or Simplicity in which they are harmonised, beyond the balanced consciousness of the indrawing and outdrawing tides.[1]

Ruysbroeck discerns three moments in this achievement. First, a negative movement, the introversive sinking-down of our created life into God's absolute life, which is the consummation of self-naughting and surrender and the essence of dark contemplation. Next, the positive ecstatic stretching forth above reason into our 'highest life,' where we undergo complete transmutation in God and feel ourselves wholly enfolded in Him. Thirdly, from these 'completing opposites' of surrender and love springs the perfect fruition of Unity, so far as we may know it here; when "we feel ourselves to be one with God, and find ourselves transformed of God, and immersed in the fathomless Abyss of our Eternal Blessedness, where we can find no further separation between ourselves and God. So long as we are lifted up and stretched forth into this height of feeling, all our powers remain idle, in an essential fruition; for where our powers are utterly naughted, there we lose our activity. And so long as we remain idle, without observation, with outstretched spirit and open eyes, so long can we see and have fruition. But in that same moment in which we would

[1] *The Book of Truth*, cap. xii.

THE SUPERESSENTIAL LIFE

test and comprehend *What* that may be which we feel, we fall back upon reason; and there we find distinction and otherness between God and ourselves, and find God as an Incomprehensible One exterior to us." [1]

It is clear from this passage that such ' utterness ' of fruition is a fleeting experience; though it is one to which the unitive mystic can return again and again, since it exists as a permanent state in his essential ground, ever discoverable by him when attention is focussed upon it. Further, it appears that the ' absence of difference ' between God and the soul, which the mystic in these moments of ecstasy feels and enjoys, is a psychological experience, not an absolute truth. It is the only way in which his surface-mind is able to realise on the one side the overwhelming apprehension of God's Love, that ' Yes ' in which all other syllables are merged; on the other the completeness of his being's self-abandonment to the Divine embrace—" that Superessential Love with which we are one, and which we possess more deeply and widely than any other thing." [2] It was for this experience that Thomas à Kempis prayed in one of his most Ruysbroeckian passages: " When shall I at full gather myself in Thee, that for Thy love I feel not myself,

[1] *The Sparkling Stone*, cap. x.
[2] *Op. cit.* cap. ix.

but Thee only, above all feeling and all manner, in a *manner not known to all?* " [1] It is to this same paradoxical victory-in-surrender—this apparent losing which is the only real finding—that Francis Thompson invites the soul:

> "To feel thyself and be
> His dear nonentity—
> Caught
> Beyond human thought
>
> In the thunder-spout of Him,
> Until thy being dim,
> And be
> Dead deathlessly."

Now here it is, in these stammered tidings of an adventure ' far outside and beyond our spirit,' in ' the darkness at which reason gazes with wide eyes,' [2] that we must look for the solution of that problem which all high mystic states involve for analytic thought: how can the human soul become one with God ' without intermediary, beyond all separation,'[3] yet remain eternally distinct from Him? How can the ' deification,' the ' union with God without differentiation' on which the great mystics insist, be accepted, and pantheism be denied?

First, we notice that in all descriptions

---

[1] *The Imitation of Christ*, lib. iii. cap. xxiii.

[2] *The Twelve Béguines*, cap. xiv., and *The Sparkling Stone*, cap. ix.

[3] *The Twelve Béguines*, cap. xvi.

of Unity given us by the mystics, there is a strong subjective element. Their first concern is always with the experience of the heart and will, not with the deductions made by the intelligence. It is at our own peril that we attach ontological meaning to their convinced and vivid psychological statements. Ruysbroeck in particular makes this quite clear to us; says again and again that he has '*felt* unity without difference and distinction,' yet that he *knows* that 'otherness' has always remained, and "that this is true we can only know by feeling it, and in no other way."[1]

In certain great moments, he says, the purified and illuminated soul which has died into God does achieve an Essential Stillness; which seems to human thought a static condition, for it is that Eternal Now of the Godhead which embraces in its span the whole process of Time. Here we find nothing but God: the naked and ultimate Fact or Superessential Being 'whence all Being has come forth,' stripped of academic trimmings and experienced in its white-hot intensity. Here, far beyond the range of thought, unity and otherness, like hunger and fulfilment, activity and rest, *can* co-exist in love. The ultimate union is a love-union, says Ruysbroeck.

[1] *The Sparkling Stone*, cap. ix.; cp. *The Book of Truth*, cap. xi.

"The Love of God is a consuming Fire, which draws us out of ourselves and swallows us up in unity with God, where we are satisfied and overflowing, and with Him, beyond ourselves, eternally fulfilled."[1]

This hungry and desirous love, at once a personal passion and a cosmic force, drenches, transfigures and unites with the soul, as sunlight does the air, as fire does the iron flung into the furnace; so that the molten metal 'changed into another glory' is both iron and fire 'ever distinct yet ever united'—an antique image of the Divine Union which he takes direct from a celebrated passage in St. Bernard's works. "As much as is iron, so much is fire; and as much as is fire, so much is iron; yet the iron doth not become fire, nor the fire iron, but each retains its substance and nature. So likewise the spirit of man doth not become God, but is deified, and knows itself breadth, length, height and depth: and as far as God is God, so far the loving spirit is made one with Him in love."[2] The iron, the air, represent our created essence; the fire, the sunlight, God's Essence, which is added to our own—our *super-essence*. The two are held in a union

---

[1] *The Twelve Béguines*, cap. xvi.
[2] *Ibid.* cap. xiv.; cp. St. Bernard, *De Diligendo Deo*, cap. x. The same image is found in St. Macarius and many other writers.

which, when we try to see it under the symbolism of space, appears a mingling, a self-mergence; but, when we feel it under the symbolism of personality, is a marriage in which the lover and beloved are 'distinct yet united.' "Then are we one being, one love, and one beatitude with God . . . a joy so great and special that we cannot even think of any other joy. For then one is one's self a Fruition of Love, and can and should want nothing beyond one's own."[1]

It follows from all this that when the soul, coming to the Fourth State of Fruitive Love, enters into the Equilibrium which supports and penetrates the flux, it does and must reconcile the opposites which have governed the earlier stages of its career. The communion reached is with a Wholeness; the life which flows from it must be a wholeness too. Full surrender, harmonised with full actualisation of all our desires and faculties; not some thin, abstract, vertical relation alone, but an all-round expansion, a full, deep, rich giving and taking, a complete correspondence with the infinitely rich, all-demanding and all-generous God whose "love is measureless for it is Himself." Thus Ruysbroeck teaches that love static and love dynamic must coexist for us as for Him; that the 'eternal hunger and thirst' of the God-

[1] *The Sparkling Stone*, cap. xii.

demanding soul continues within its ecstatic satisfaction; because, however deeply it may love and understand, the Divine Excess will always baffle it. It is destined 'ever to go forward within the Essence of God,' to grow without ceasing deeper and deeper into this life, in "the eternal longing to follow after and attain Him Who is measureless." "And we learn this truth from His sight: that all we taste, in comparison with that which remains out of our reach, is no more than a single drop of water compared with the whole sea. . . . We hunger for God's Infinity, which we cannot devour, and we aspire to His Eternity, which we cannot attain. . . . In this storm of love, our activity is above reason and is in no wise. Love desires that which is impossible to her; and reason teaches that love is within her rights, but can neither counsel nor persuade her."[1]

Hence an eternal desire and an eternal satisfaction are preserved within the circle of the deified life. The full-grown self feels, in its most intense degree, the double movement of the Divine Love and Light, the flux and reflux; and in its perfect and ever-renewed responses to the 'indrawing and outflowing attraction' of that Tide, the complete possession of the Superessential Life consists.

[1] *The Sparkling Stone*, cap. x.

"The indrawing attraction drags us out of ourselves, and calls us to be melted away and naughted in the Unity. And in this indrawing attraction we feel that God wills that we should be His, and for this we must abnegate ourselves and let our beatitude be accomplished in Him. But when He attracts us by flowing out towards us, He gives us over to ourselves and makes us free, and sets us in Time."[1]

Thus is accomplished that parodoxical synthesis of 'Eternal Rest and Eternal Work' which Ruysbroeck regards as the essential character of God, and towards which the whole of his system has been educating the human soul. The deified or 'God-formed' soul is for him the spirit in which this twofold ideal is actualised: this is the Pattern, the Likeness of God, declared in Christ our Archetype, towards which the Indwelling Spirit presses the race. Though there are moments in which, carried away as it seems by his almost intolerable ecstasy, he pushes out towards 'that unwalled Fruition of God,' where all fruition begins and ends, where 'one is all and all is one,' and Man is himself a 'fruition of love';[2] yet he never forgets to remind us that, as love is not love unless it looks forward towards the creation of new life,

[1] *The Sparkling Stone*, cap. x.
[2] *Op. cit.* cap. xii.

so here, "when love falls in love with love, and each is all to the other in possession and in rest," the *object* of this ecstasy is not a permanent self-loss in the Divine Darkness, a 'slumbering in God,' but a "new life of virtue, such as love and its impulses demand."[1] "To be a living, willing Tool of God, wherewith God works what He will and how He will," is the goal of transcendence described in the last chapter of *The Sparkling Stone.* "Then is our life a *whole*, when contemplation and work dwell in us side by side, and we are perfectly in both of them at once";[2] for then the separate spirit is immersed in, and part of, the perpetual creative act of the Godhead—the flowing forth and the drawing back, which have at their base the Eternal Equilibrium, the unbroken peace, wherein "God contemplates Himself and all things in an Eternal Now that has neither beginning nor end."[3] On that Unbroken Peace the spirit hangs; and swings like a pendulum, in wide arcs of love and service, between the Unconditioned and the Conditioned Worlds.

So the Superessential Life is the simple, the synthetic life, in which man actualises at last all the resources of his complex being.

---

[1] *Op. cit.* cap. xiii. ; cp. also *The Seven Degrees*, cap. xiv.
[2] *The Sparkling Stone*, cap. xiv.
[3] *The Spiritual Marriage*, lib. iii. cap. v.

THE SUPERESSENTIAL LIFE

The active life of response to the Temporal Order, the contemplative life of response to the Transcendent Order are united, firmly held together, by that 'eternal fixation of the spirit'; the perpetual willed dwelling of the being of man within the Incomprehensible Abyss of the Being of God, *qui est per omnia saecula benedictus.*

BIBLIOGRAPHICAL NOTE

I. Flemish Text

Werken van Jan van Ruusbroec. Ed. J. DAVID.
6 vols. (Maetschappy der Vlaemsche Bibliophilen). (Gent, 1858–68.)

This edition, based on the MSS. preserved at Brussels and Ghent, and the foundation of all the best translations, is now rare. It may be consulted at the British Museum.

A re-issue of the Flemish text is now in progress; the first volume being *Jan van Ruysbroeck, Van den VII. Trappen* (i.e. *The Seven Degrees of Love*) *met Geert Groote's latijnsche Vertaling.* Ed. Dom. Ph. MÜLLER (Brussels, 1911).

II. Translations

A. *Latin*

The chief works of Ruysbroeck were early translated into Latin, some during their author's lifetime, and widely circulated in this form. Three of these early translations were printed in the sixteenth century: the *De Ornatu Spiritualium Nuptiarum* of Jordaens, at Paris, in 1512; and the *De Septem Scalæ Divini Amoris Gradibus* of Gerard

Groot, together with the *De Perfectione Filiorum Dei* (i.e. *The Sparkling Stone*), at Bologna, in 1538.

The standard Latin translation, however—indispensable to all students of Ruysbroeck—is the great work of the Carthusian monk, LAURENTIUS SURIUS: *D. Joannis Rusbrochii Opera Omnia* (Cologne, 1552).

This was reprinted in 1609 (the best edition), and again in 1692. It contains all Ruysbroeck's authentic works, and some that are doubtful; in a translation singularly faithful to the sense of the original, though it fails to reproduce the rugged sublimity, the sudden lapses into crude and homely metaphor, so characteristic of his style.

B. *English*

The Book of the Twelve Béguines (the first sixteen chapters only). Translated from the Flemish, by JOHN FRANCIS (London, 1913).

A useful translation of one of Ruysbroeck's most difficult treatises.

C. *French*

Œuvres de Ruysbroeck l'Admirable. Traduction du Flamand par les BÉNÉDICTINS DE SAINT PAUL DE WISQUES.
    VOL. I.: *Le Miroir du Salut Éternel; Les Sept Clôtures; Les Sept Degrés de l'Échelle d'Amour Spirituel* (Brussels, 1912, in progress).

This edition, when completed, will form the standard text of Ruysbroeck for those unable to read Flemish. The translation is admirably lucid, and a short but adequate introduction is prefixed to each work.

L'Ornement des Noces Spirituelles. Traduit du Flamand par MAURICE MAETERLINCK (Brussels, 1900).

This celebrated book, still more its beautiful though unreliable introduction, is chiefly responsible for the modern interest in Ruysbroeck. The translation, exquisite as French prose, overemphasises the esoteric element in his teaching. Those unable to read Flemish should check it by LAMBERT's German text (see below).

Vie de Rusbroch suivie de son Traité des Sept Degrés de l'Amour. Traduction littérale du Texte Flamand-Latin, par R. CHAMONAL (Paris, 1909). *Traité du Royaume des Amants de Dieu.* Traduit par R. CHAMONAL (Paris, 1911). *De la Vraie Contemplation* (i.e. *The Twelve Béguines*). Traduit par R. CHAMONAL. 3 vols. (Paris, 1912).

These are the first volumes of a proposed complete translation; which is, however, far from literal, and replaces the rough vigour of the original by the insipid language of conventional French piety.

Livre des XII. Béguines ou de la Vraie Contemplation (first sixteen chapters only). Traduit du Flamand, avec Introduction, par L'ABBÉ P. CUYLITS (Brussels, 1909).

This also contains a French version of the *Vita* of Pomerius. The translator is specially successful in rendering the peculiar quality of Ruysbroeck's verse; but the statements in his introduction must be accepted with reserve.

D. *German*

Drei Schriften des Mystikers Johann van Ruysbroeck, aus dem Vlämischen übersetzt von FRANZ A. LAMBERT (Leipzig, 1902).

A vigorous and accurate translation of *The Adornment of the Spiritual Marriage, The Sparkling Stone* and *The Book of Supreme Truth.*

Ruysbroeck translates better into German than into any other language; and this volume is strongly recommended to all who can read that tongue.

III. SELECTIONS

Rusbrock l'Admirable: Œuvres Choisies. Traduit par E. HELLO (Paris, 1902).

A series of short passages, paraphrased (*not* translated) from the Latin of Surius. There are two English versions of this unsatisfactory book, the second being the best:

Reflections from the Mirror of a Mystic. Translated by EARLE BAILLIE (London, 1905).

Flowers of a Mystic Garden. Translated by C. E. S. (London, 1912).

Life, Light, and Love: Selections from the German Mystics. By the Very Rev. W. R. INGE, D.D., Dean of St. Paul's (London, 1905).

Contains an abridged version of *The Adornment of the Spiritual Marriage.*

Biography and Criticism

(A Selection)

AUGER, A.—*De Doctrina et Meritis Joannis van Ruysbroeck* (Louvain, 1892).

ENGELHARDT, J. G. VON.—*Richard von St. Victor und J. Ruysbroeck* (Erlangen, 1838).
Useful for tracing the correspondences between the Victorines and Ruysbroeck.

MAETERLINCK, MAURICE.—*Ruysbroeck and the Mystics.* Translated by JANE STODDART (London, 1908).
An English version of the Introduction to *L'Ornement des Noces Spirituelles*, above-mentioned; with many fine passages translated from Ruysbroeck's other works.

POMERIUS, H.—*De Origine Monasterii Viridisvallis una cum Vitis Joannis Rusbrochii.*
Printed in *Analecta Bollandiana*, vol. iv. (Brussels, 1885). The chief authority for all biographical facts.

SCULLY, Dom VINCENT.—*A Mediæval Mystic* (London, 1910).
A biographical account, founded on Pomerius, with a short analysis of Ruysbroeck's works. Popular and uncritical.

VREESE, Dr. W. L. DE.—*Jean de Ruysbroeck* (*Biographie Nationale de Belgique*, vol. xx.) (Brussels, 1907).
An important and authoritative article with

analysis of all Ruysbroeck's works and full bibliography.

—— *Bijdragen tot de Kennis van het Leven en de Werken van Jan van Ruusbroec* (Gent, 1896).
Contains Gerard Naghel's sketch of Ruysbroeck's life, with other useful material.

—— *De Handschriften van Jan van Ruusbroec's Werken.* 2 vols. (Gent, 1900).
An important and scholarly study of the manuscript sources by the greatest living authority.

Notices of Ruysbroeck will be found in the following works :—

AUGER, A.—*Étude sur les Mystiques des Pays Bas au Moyen Age* (*Académie Royale de Belgique*, vol. xlvi., 1892).

FLEMING, W. K.—*Mysticism in Christianity* (London, 1913).

INGE, Very Rev. W. R., D.D., Dean of St. Paul's.—*Christian Mysticism* (London, 1899).

JONES, Dr. RUFUS M.—*Studies in Mystical Religion* (London, 1909).

Applications of his doctrine to the spiritual life in :—

BAKER, Venerable AUGUSTIN.—*Holy Wisdom; or Directions for the Prayer of Contemplation* (London, 1908).

BLOSIUS, F. V.—*Book of Spiritual Instruction* (London, 1900); *A Mirror for Monks* (London, 1901); *Comfort for the Faint-hearted* (London, 1903); *Sanctuary of the Faithful Soul* (London, 1905).

DENIS THE CARTHUSIAN.—*Opera Omnia* (Monstrolii, 1896), in progress.

BIBLIOGRAPHICAL NOTE

PETERSEN, GERLAC. — *The Fiery Soliloquy with God* (London, 1872).

POULAIN, AUG., S.J.—*The Graces of Interior Prayer* (London, 1910).

UNDERHILL, E.—*Mysticism*, 5th ed. (London, 1914).

INFLUENCES

Much light is thrown on Ruysbroeck's doctrine by a study of the authors who influenced him; especially:

ST. AUGUSTINE; MIGNE, *P.L.*, xxvii.–xlvii.; Eng. Trans., edited by M. DODS (Edinburgh, 1876).

DIONYSIUS THE AREOPAGITE; MIGNE, *P.G.*, iii., iv.; Eng. Trans., by PARKER (Oxford, 1897).

HUGH and RICHARD OF ST. VICTOR; MIGNE, *P.L.*, clxxv.–clxxvii. and cxcvi.

ST. BERNARD; MIGNE, *P.L.*, clxxxii.–clxxxv.; Eng. Trans., by EALES (London, 1889–96).

ST. THOMAS AQUINAS; *Opera* (Romæ, 1882–1906); Eng. Trans., by the DOMINICAN FATHERS (in progress).

ST. BONAVENTURA; *Opera* (Paris, 1864–71).

Meister ECKHART; *Schriften und Predigten* (Leipzig, 1903).

SUSO; *Schriften*, ed. DENIFLE (Munich, 1876). Eng. Trans., *Life*, ed. by W. R. INGE (London, 1913); *Book of Eternal Wisdom* (London, 1910).

TAULER, *Predigten* (Prague, 1872); Eng. Trans., *Twenty-five Sermons*, trans. by WINKWORTH (London, 1906); *The Inner Way*, edited by A. W. HUTTON (London, 1909).

Printed by
MORRISON & GIBB LIMITED
Edinburgh

Demy 8vo. 7s. 6d. net.

QUESTS
OLD AND NEW

By G. R. S. MEAD

EDITOR OF 'THE QUEST SERIES'

AUTHOR OF 'THRICE-GREATEST HERMES,' 'FRAGMENTS
OF A FAITH FORGOTTEN,' ETC. ETC.

CONTENTS

THE WAY OF THE SPIRIT IN ANCIENT CHINA.
THE DOCTRINE OF THE TRUE MAN IN ANCIENT CHINESE MYSTICAL PHILOSOPHY.
SPIRITUAL REALITY IN PROGRESSIVE BUDDHISM.
THE IDEAL LIFE IN PROGRESSIVE BUDDHISM.
SOME FEATURES OF BUDDHIST PSYCHOLOGY.
THE DOCTRINE OF REINCARNATION ETHICALLY CONSIDERED.
SOME MYSTICAL EXPERIMENTS ON THE FRONTIERS OF EARLY CHRISTENDOM.
THE MEANING OF GNOSIS IN THE HIGHER FORMS OF HELLENISTIC RELIGION.
'THE BOOK OF THE HIDDEN MYSTERIES,' BY HIEROTHEOS.
THE RISING PSYCHIC TIDE.
VAIHINGER'S PHILOSOPHY OF THE 'AS IF.'
BERGSON'S INTUITIONISM.
EUCKEN'S ACTIVISM.

LONDON: G. BELL AND SONS LTD.

THE MISSING GODDESS, AND OTHER LEGENDS

BY

MINNIE B. THEOBALD.

Crown 8vo. 3s. net.

THESE allegorical stories, written by a musician, form a distinct contribution to the literature of experimental psychology. The authoress claims that they were actually written in a state of exaltation induced by long and intense concentration on musical exercises. Fresh in style, graphic and original in character, they deal with those problems in this world and the next which are of vital interest to all, and will make special appeal to students of the psychology of different phases of consciousness.

RALPH WALDO TRINE'S NEW BOOK

THE NEW ALINEMENT OF LIFE

Post 8vo. 3s. 6d. net.

THE author's main object in this new volume is to sift out the fundamental truths of **real Christianity.** He separates them from the many half-truths and errors which nowadays so often overlay them. It will appeal to all thoughtful readers, expressing as it does the very ideas so many of us have tried to express. Like all Mr. Trine's books, it will inspire to better living and better thinking, and shows what a little wholesome philosophy will do toward the attainment of true happiness.

LONDON: G. BELL AND SONS LTD.